We Made It Through
The Winter

We Made It Through The Winter

A Memoir of
Northern Minnesota Boyhood

by
Walter O'Meara

MINNESOTA HISTORICAL SOCIETY · ST. PAUL · 1974

Copyright © 1974 by the MINNESOTA HISTORICAL SOCIETY

First paperback printing, 1986
International Standard Book Number 0-87351-212-X
Manufactured in the United States of America
10   9   8   7   6   5   4   3   2   1

Library of Congress Cataloging in Publication Data

O'Meara, Walter.
   We made it through the winter: a memoir of north-
ern Minnesota boyhood.
   (Publications of the Minnesota Historical
Society)
   1. O'Meara, Walter — Biography. I. Title.
II. Series: Minnesota Historical Society. Pub-
lications. PS3529.M4Z527   813'.5'2 [B]   74-18369

For my children,
my grandchildren, and
the "greats" who are now
coming along

About the Author

ALTHOUGH he was born in Minneapolis, Walter O'Meara spent his entire boyhood and youth in Cloquet, Minnesota. He was graduated from Cloquet High School and attended the University of Minnesota for a year, after which he transferred to the University of Wisconsin School of Journalism.

Following World War I, in which he served as an artillery sergeant, Mr. O'Meara worked for a year as a reporter on the *Duluth News-Tribune*, then returned to the University of Wisconsin. He was graduated in 1920 with Phi Beta Kappa honors.

For the next five decades Mr. O'Meara varied a highly successful business career with the writing of history and fiction. His fifteen published books, including two best-selling novels, have reflected his special interest in the Canadian and American fur trade and in American Indian life. He himself is an adopted member of the Lac Court Oreilles (Wisconsin) band of Chippewa.

During World War II, Mr. O'Meara served as chief of the planning staff in the Office of Strategic Services and as deputy price administrator in charge of OPA's department of information. He was director of all media publicity for Adlai Stevenson in his 1956 presidential campaign. In 1957 he received a citation for distinguished services in journalism from the University of Wisconsin.

Since retiring from business, Mr. O'Meara and his wife, Esther Arnold O'Meara, have lived much of the time in Arizona, close to the Mexican border. There he wrote his latest book, *Daughters of the Country* (1968), a study of Indian women on the white man's frontier. He is now at work on a novel tentatively entitled "The Last Padre," based on the Jesuit expulsion.

Mr. O'Meara and his wife of fifty-two years have four children, fourteen grandchildren, and three great-grand-children living in Connecticut, New York, South Carolina, Michigan, England, Brazil, and Venezuela. "I thought it might help to pull the scattered sept together if the Old Man wrote a book about his boyhood," Mr. O'Meara says. "And this is it."

Acknowledgments

I WISH to thank my sister, Helen Hilger, for helping me to recall many pleasant aspects of our life at home — like that bean pot at the back of our Radiant Home Base Burner. And Kathryn Elfes Gray, whose delightful reminiscences in the *Cloquet Vidette* from May 3 to October 23, 1967, reminded me of such long forgotten bits of color as Gilbert's train and Pants Mary. And June D. Holmquist, assistant director of the Minnesota Historical Society, who with Alan Ominsky, Bruce M. White, and Carolyn Gilman of her staff contributed invaluable editorial and research assistance in preparing my little book for the printers.

And not least, my thanks to my dear wife Esther and to my children, Donn, Ellen, Deirdre, and Wolfe, for prodding me into writing this rambling account of how things were "way back in those days."

The family portraits that appear between pages 20 and 21 are from my personal collection. All the other photographs and illustrations in the book are from the audio-visual library of the Minnesota Historical Society.

Walter O'Meara

Contents

CHAPTER ONE

Wonders and Marvels, 1906

Tom Mogan had suffered a bad stroke,[1] and every Sunday morning after Mass my father dropped by to see how his old chum was getting along. Once when I was ten years old he took me with him.

"This is my boy, Walter," my father said. "He is my oldest."

Old Tom could move only his eyes and the muscles of his mouth a little, but he managed a faint smile of greeting. Then his gaze shifted to a short-stemmed pipe — the kind lumberjacks called a nose warmer — on the bedside table.

My father nodded and filled the pipe with strong, black tobacco from a paper of Peerless. He placed it carefully in Old Tom's mouth and adjusted a kind of sling he had contrived to support the bowl. He struck a match, and soon Old Tom had his pipe going.

"Well, Mike," he whispered, after a few contented puffs, "what is the news?"

Great crowds in New York had welcomed William Jennings Bryan home from his trip around the world, my father told him. Joe Gans had beat Battling Nelson in forty-two rounds. Joseph Glidden, inventor of the barbed-wire fence, had died. Dan Patch had paced the mile in 1:55.[2]

But soon the talk turned from news of the world and great events, and they spoke of the woods. My father wiped the drool from Old Tom's chin and waited for him to speak, for it was plain he wished to say something.

"Mike," Old Tom asked haltingly in a queer, faraway voice, "Mike, do ye mind the time Kelsey took out ten million feet of pine on the Embarrass?"

1

"I do, Tom," my father said. "It was in the winter of eighteen and ninety-six."

"All clear white pine," Old Tom whispered.

"And not a stick that didn't scale five hundred feet," my father remembered.

"Aye, fifty feet they went to the crown, them fellers," Old Tom said in his slow, difficult speech.

He puffed a few times at his pipe, while his dim gray eyes lit up with his memories. Then, in a voice of sudden, startling strength, he said, "By God, Mike, that was timber!"

Timber. It was the lifestuff of the small northern Minnesota town in which I grew to manhood. It was the source and support of everything useful and good. The people of that town thought timber, talked timber, labored with it in the deep woods and steam-driven mills, and sometimes gave their lives to it in the somber forest or on the white-water streams. They spent their lives from youth to old age in the cutting, driving, and sawing of timber. And all my boyhood memories are suffused with the fragrance of new-cut pine, the ceaseless hum and vibration of the great sawmills, the talk of logging camps and log drives.

Small towns in the Middle West have short memories, and nobody knew how ours had got its name. But even that may have been derived from the timber. At first a little cluster of log houses on the St. Louis River had been called Knife Falls, from the rapids just below the village. Then, in the 1870s, a sawmill was built, and a little later the name was changed to Cloquet. Scholars have conjectured that this is a corruption of the French *claquet*, an echoic word for the sound made by the water-driven mill. Early settlers, however, held to a belief that the town was named for a missionary priest, Father Cloquet.[3]

With plenty of white pine and water power with which to cut it, Cloquet boomed. The lumber barons from downstate moved in and built more and bigger mills. Soon five mills,[4] supplied with logs from forty-odd camps, shivered and screeched day and night, ripping through sawlogs, spewing out lumber. Cloquet, with frontier ebullience, proclaimed itself "The White Pine Capital of the World." Or sometimes, "The Queen City of the St. Louis."

It would never end. The supply of timber, everyone said, was inexhaustible. The demand for lumber from the burgeoning cities of the south was insatiable. Our town basked in typical Middle Border security: it had not one worry about the future. For who could dream that men then living would saw Cloquet's last log and hear the mills fall silent forever? In 1906 there was still plenty of pine, and plenty of work, and times were good. For a boy of ten, they were indeed very good.

Tending to cluster around the mother mills, Cloquet divided itself into two parts named for the major mill operators: Nelsontown and Shawtown. On the river flats stood the sawmills, lumberyards, and most of the town's large buildings, such as the company stores, boardinghouses for the single mill hands, horse barns, and warehouses. The rest of the town sprawled over a hillside looking northward across the river. On the western outskirts, a few French Canadians lived in a cluster of small houses, all painted bright blue, called "Little Canada" or "Bluetown." The wealthy millowners — what the *Pine Knot,* our weekly newspaper, called "the lumber company aristocracy" — occupied the exclusive heights of Chestnut Hill. It was a neighborhood we seldom ventured into.[5]

For a mill town, there were not many "company houses" in Cloquet. Most were built by the owners themselves, often with the help of neighbors. Each had its tiny front yard, with a bit of lawn and a flower bed under the windows, and a back yard with a vegetable garden, potato patch, woodshed, privy, and perhaps a henhouse or even a cowshed. Along the unpaved streets a few trees, mostly maples and box elders, had grown tall enough to shade the gravel walks. There was nothing quaint or charming about our town, I am afraid; not even anything crude or ugly enough to render it remarkable. But in at least a couple of respects it was unique.

For one thing, Cloquet was built entirely of wood. It was a wholly *wooden* town. "Wood was, and remains, one of the essential substances of the world," it has been said. "It must once have appeared to some men as *the* substance."[6] And so, indeed, it must have appeared to the people of our town. For every single house in Cloquet was of frame construction. So were the larger and grander buildings, some of quite immense size, such as the Northern Lumber Company's store, the sawmills, and the Catholic church. In Cloquet wood was everywhere you looked. It choked the St. Louis River from bank to bank in the form of sawlogs. It was piled high along the river in endless stacks of sawed lumber, towering row on row, forming a sort of wooden city in itself, with plank-paved streets and grassy alleys between the stacks. All the sidewalks in Cloquet were of wood, deep-pitted by the calks of rivermen's driving boots. The water tanks, horse troughs, and wagon and sleigh boxes were wood. So were the fences, and you could walk all over town, practically, on the top rails. Piles and piles of firewood were stacked in back yards to stoke kitchen ranges. Wood, indeed, met the eye in all directions, and the smell of fresh-cut lumber drifted over the town on every breeze from the river.

The other unusual thing about Cloquet, I am forced to admit, was the Island. On the maps it was Dunlap Island, but everyone called it simply "the Island." You reached it over a trussed iron bridge that had once been painted barn red. Its flooring of loose boards made a plankety-plank sound when a wagon or buggy drove over it. Sometimes we ventured onto the bridge, but we must never cross over it. For the Island was no fit place for a curious small boy to visit. No woman — at least none who valued her reputation — ever went near it. And a respectable citizen drew the curtains of his buggy when he drove across the bridge in broad daylight.

There was only one street on the Island, and there was nothing on this street but fourteen saloons, with their dickey fronts and murky windows staring across a broad plank sidewalk toward the river. The city fathers had thought it best to segregate the drinking of hard liquor to the Island, and they had probably acted wisely. For when the camps broke in the spring and Cloquet suddenly swarmed with a horde of lumberjacks turned loose after a long, dry winter in the woods, it was just as well that their frolics be surrounded by deep water.

What happened on the Island was not a small boy's business,

but some stories of the colorful doings "over there" reached our young ears; and I remember especially my Uncle Dan telling of a lumberjack called Big Jake. Big Jake made local history by vaulting onto the bar of McCarthy's saloon and waltzing down its length kicking off the customers' glasses and bellowing "Protestant Boys."[7] To make matters worse, this took place on St. Patrick's Day. My Uncle Dan, who often described this historic event, would always finish his story with: "Big Jake performed this rash act, to be sure, in the spring of nineteen ought three. May his soul rest in peace."

In general, the townspeople tolerated the Island's lurid goings-on in exchange for relative peace on their own side of the river. There was a local tradition, however, that in 1903 a band of irate women stormed the Island and burned down one of the saloons. Or, in another version of the story that never quite made sense to us kids, it was a mysterious house on the hill beyond the river.

While things may have been lively enough at the other end of the red iron bridge, the course of daily life in Cloquet itself was not very eventful. Around the year 1906 nothing that occurred there ever made headlines, except in the *Pine Knot*. We were, to tell the truth, a small, rough, and no doubt very dull town. At least for grown-ups.

All through the summer the men of Cloquet worked for ten or twelve hours a day in the mills, or piling cut lumber, or shoving logs on the river. But the summers were short — "eight months of winter and four of poor sledding," people joked, a little grimly. By Thanksgiving the endless season of dark days and subarctic cold had set in. When ice formed in the millponds, the shriek of the band saws slicing through sawlogs ceased. The mill whistles summoning the crews to work and sending the night shifts home died away. And a long wintery silence settled over our town.

Then, as logging operations began in the woods, the men slung their packs on their backs and left for the camps. By Christmas most of them were gone, leaving their women and children to wait out the winter in a half-empty town. When the camps broke in the spring, they returned, with the log drive on their heels, bringing the winter's cut of timber to the waiting saws. And once again the strident whistles of the mills reverberated over the town, calling all hands back to work.

So the years turned in Cloquet, each very like the one before, since change came slowly in those far-off days and the tempo of life was deliberate, if not downright plodding. For this was a long lifetime before anyone had loped across the astonished surface of the moon. Nobody had yet listened to a radio or sat staring at a television set, and there were no movies to speak of — at least in Cloquet. Nobody in our town knew what it was like to go up in an airplane. Very few had ever bumped over the dirt streets of Cloquet in an automobile. And hardly anyone except the rich people on Chestnut Hill had a telephone, electric lights, running water, or central heating.

Our parents lacked most of the small conveniences and amenities of later times. No wristwatches, safety razors, flashlights, or ball-point pens. I cannot recall anything made of plastic, unless it was Celluloid articles, including men's collars and cuffs and the Bakelite bit of my Uncle Will's pipe. Aluminum was the new "miracle metal," and I remember marveling at the incredible lightness of an aluminum cooking pot. Zippers were a newly invented device for closing the plackets of women's skirts, what else?

But a small boy does not miss what he has never known or even imagined. So we did not feel deprived of cold cereals for breakfast, peanut butter and jelly sandwiches, ice cream cones, bubble gum, and Koolaid — let alone Mickey Mouse watches, transistor radios, and comic books. Besides, we had our own special blessings that more than made up, I think, for what we lacked. We could snare rabbits in the snowy muskegs and fish for trout in Otter Creek. We could make slip-whistles from the willows in spring and hockey sticks from swamp alder saplings. We found blueberries, raspberries, and hazelnuts in the cutover, and cranberries lying on the moss in Tamarack Swamp. We "ran logs" on the St. Louis River and swam in its cool brown water. We did a great many things that no boy in any city or suburb can ever know about today, and it seems to me we did not find life very dull.

Indeed, I cannot rid myself of the notion that it was a life filled with wonders and marvels. Of course, a small boy's eyes, no less than an old man's memory, may be mistrusted. And so the St. Louis River may not have been nearly so wide as I remember it, nor the steeple of the Catholic church so high, nor the creamy thunderheads so towering in the cobalt Minnesota sky. The arbutus may not have been quite so fragrant in May, nor the snows so deep in winter, nor little Sally Dahl, who sat two seats ahead of me in the fifth grade, half so pretty. I can tell you about Cloquet only as a boy knew it and an old man remembers it. And who can say for certain that I do not remember it truly?

CHAPTER TWO

They Followed the Pine

Now that I have told you about our town and how it came to be on the map, a small dot about fifteen miles due west of the tip of Lake Superior, I shall say a word about the people who lived there. And first the Indians.

The Fond du Lac Reservation was not far from town, and sometimes on a summer day we would take the old tote road that ran along the bank of the St. Louis River until we came to it. We never ventured far into the reservation. The great Dakota or Sioux Outbreak of 1862 was still remembered by old-timers, and people who did not know our own Chippewa or Ojibway Indians very well did not quite trust them. So our mothers warned us not to go beyond black-bearded Father Simon Lampe's little mission church at the boundary of the Indian lands.[1]

The first Indian I remember was Suzy Posey, who did our washing. I still have a vivid memory of her hanging out the sheets on a windy day, a very small woman with a battered black hat on her head and a corncob pipe in her mouth. After a while, Suzy was followed by a young Indian girl who once stole a pair of my mother's earrings and showed up the following week wearing them. After scolding her gently, my mother said to my sisters and me with, I am sure, no pejorative intent, "She really didn't mean to do anything bad — it's just the way she is."

The only Indian boy I played with was one who lived in our neighborhood, Nidji Cadreau, and I believe he became a pitcher for the Chicago White Sox when he grew up and left Cloquet.[2] Nidji's father had a decrepit birch-bark canoe under the gooseberry bushes along his back fence. One summer's

8

day, with nothing more constructive to do, we embarked on a canoe-renovating project. Under Nidji's expert direction we all worked diligently for a couple of days, patching and gumming the ancient craft. Then we carried it down to Pinehurst Park and launched it on Skinn Lake, where it immediately sank with Nidji in it.

A few other Indian people lived in Cloquet itself. Among them were the La Prairie brothers, Henry and John, famous as rivermen and birlers (log rollers).[3] And Mike Houle, also a riverman, who played first base on the Cloquet baseball team. He won immortality by blasting a home run into the Protestant graveyard in the climactic game of the season with the neighboring town of Proctor.

↟

After the Indians came the loggers. Some of them had followed the white pine across half a continent, from Maine to New York, from New York to Pennsylvania, then to the Upper Peninsula of Michigan and west to Wisconsin. All they knew was how to whack down trees and saw them into lumber. Now they were happily letting daylight into the swamps of northern Minnesota. Mostly they were Scotch, Irish, and down-East Yankees of the same leathery breed, celebrated by my good friend Stewart Holbrook in *Holy Old Mackinaw,* who had driven the Penobscot and pounded the bars of Bangor. Among the Swedes, Finns, and French Canadians who later infiltrated the logging world, they were the elite, the boss loggers, timber cruisers, top loaders, drive foremen. And they gave pride of place to no man.[4]

In a sawmill town a boy listened to his elders tell stories about the woods and rivers — "stove logging," they called it — and of famous camp bosses and their exploits. To this day, I have not forgotten their names: Jack Chisholm, Duncan Cameron, John Cordy, Hank Allen, Dinny Boyle, Johnny Long, Mike Sullivan, Charlie Keller, Tom Lynch, Ed Netser, Percy Vibert, Nick Sloan, Terry Lynch, Scotty Boyle, George Dixon, Bill Carter, and Bill Bradley. There were others, less prestigious, perhaps, but by no means less interesting: Mushhead Higgins, for instance, the Whiteface Liar, Overland Daley, Dangling

Jones the Mancatcher, Beefslough Flannigan, Roothouse Pete, Johnnie-on-the-Spot, the Galloping Twins, and Crosshaul Carlson.

On a Sunday afternoon a small boy might listen to his father and a chum recall the deeds of famous loggers. How, in the winter of 1907, Johnny Long, with a crew of a hundred men, landed nine million feet of pine on Bug Creek without any proper landing, simply skidding the logs into three miles of the creek, then driving them down the Bug, the Whiteface, and the St. Louis to the mill at Cloquet.[5] The boy might not grasp the nuances of Johnny's unorthodox style of logging, but he would always think of Johnny Long as a celebrated camp boss, to be forever remembered and admired.

Then there was Scotty Boyle, who logged the Embarrass River. In Scotty's camp, my father said, the crew was not awakened, as in other camps, by the raucous notes of the long tin horn called the "gabrel." No indeed. "Give 'em 'Larry,'" Scotty would say to a young Irishman on his crew, and the men were apprised of the dawn of a new day in the pines by the sweet strains of "Larry O'Sullivan."[6]

In this way, too, I learned about the Big Sister and the Little Sister, who went with the tote teams from camp to camp in their nuns' habits, and sometimes on snowshoes, selling hospital tickets to the lumberjacks.[7] And how Mushhead Higgins lost his whole crew because he insisted on cutting "popple" (poplar or aspen), a practice that was sure to bring death to his camp. And about the night the barn cats got into Paddy Hogan's cook shanty and made off with the Christmas turkeys.

It was a rare lumberjack, indeed, who did not have a story to tell for a small boy's wonderment, perhaps a personal experience, or maybe a tale that had long made the rounds of the camps to become folklore at last. And among them, of course, were the Paul Bunyan stories.[8]

Paul, as you must know, was the legendary camp boss who logged the Pyramid Forty in the winter of the blue snows — with the help of Babe, his blue ox who measured exactly six ax handles and a plug of Climax chewing tobacco between the horns. After logging all four sides of the Pyramid Forty in snow so deep that his sawing crews left forty-foot stumps, Paul landed his cut on the Big Onion River. When the ice broke in the spring, the drive began. After a while it passed a set of camps that had a somehow familiar look. Then another. And it was not until the third time around that Paul realized the camps were his own: the Big Onion flowed round and round the Pyramid Forty without an outlet!

The Paul Bunyan stories were always told straight-faced, and usually began, "I remember the winter I went up for Paul. . . ." But I can still see the twinkle in one old logger's eyes when he told me of Paul's last, long trek toward the setting sun. Having logged the Dakotas so clean that not a sign of any stump remained, Paul headed west with Babe and his crew, climbed to the summit of the Cascade Range, and looked down on the shining waters of the Pacific Ocean. "And there, to be sure, he saw Old Puget building the Sound."

The lore of the camps created a kind of "second world" for a small boy in a sawmill town — a world separate and apart, yet very real. It was the remote, mysterious, fascinating world into which his father disappeared each winter, and to which he himself would someday go. There was logger's blood in all of us, and so we listened to the tales of camps and drives with a special, personal interest, longing for the time when we, too, would "go up in the woods."

The loggers, so to speak, begat Cloquet, but the French Canadians were actually on the scene long before them. As early as 1800 the *voyageurs* from Lower Canada were lugging their big north canoes around Knife Falls. And a roster of North West Company canoemen for that year is reminiscent of a list of Cloquet's French-Canadian families in 1906: Bouche, Beaupre, Roy (Roi), Paul-Joseph, Loisel, Chartier, Bernier, La Vasseur, La Tulip, Brouseau, de la Rushe, Cyrette (Sarette), Le Fleur, Chapados.[9]

Cloquet's French Canadians were from the province of Quebec, from the little towns along the St. Lawrence with the lovely names: Varennes, Sorel, Contrecoeur, St. Hyacinthe, Gentilly, Ste. Victorie, Cap de Madelaine. Like the Yankee loggers, they had followed the pine far from home, but they had not lost all their ancestral ways. There was much visiting back and forth among them on New Year's Day, with wine and kisses for men and women alike. A *potage* of dried peas and pork was a favorite dish, as it had been with the *habitants*. And newly married couples were still subjected to the ancient and harrowing ordeal of the noisy charivari.

Because our French Canadians liked to hear and speak their native tongue, it was customary in the Cloquet Catholic church to have a French priest and for the sermon to be preached in French and English on alternate Sundays. To his English-speaking parishioners, however, Father Charles Giraux's sermons always sounded like pure French, and finally they summoned courage to petition the bishop in Duluth for his removal. Shortly afterward lightning struck the tall steeple of the church of Our Lady of the Sacred Heart, and it burned to the ground.[10] Good Father Giraux never really implied that Somebody Up There was less than pleased with his fickle flock, but he never discouraged the idea either.

Although our French Canadians themselves tended to perpetuate a certain ethnic separateness, I cannot recall anything like tension between them and the rest of us. We never — well, almost never — called them "Frogs" or "Canucks." Perhaps we did mimic their French patois, but we did so more in amusement than in ridicule. And the very small fry sometimes sang a mildly derisive ballad that went:

> Pea soup and johnnycake
> Make a Frenchman's belly ache.

But most of the French-Canadian kids were, like their old men, remarkably strong, quick, and agile, and it was just as well to be careful about offending their sensibilities.

"Give me enough Swedes and snuff," James J. Hill is supposed to have said, "and I could build a railroad to the moon." He did import a good many Scandinavians to lay the transcontinental tracks of his Great Northern Railway, and some of them overflowed into the sawmills and lumberyards of our town. Naturally their ties with the Old Country were strong. Many Swedish families had a framed picture of King Oscar II hanging in their front parlors. A rather large number spoke little English.

My earliest friend — I was still wearing dresses, which was how they dressed very little boys in those days — was a small boy named Carl Bruno.[11] We got along very well on a two-language basis. It took no Norwegian on my part and no English on his for us to plan a trip to the other end of town — where we were found by our anxious parents sitting on the railroad track, no doubt plotting further adventures.

I remember Carl's mother as a handsome blonde woman whose kitchen was fragrant with the delicious smells of fresh bread and coffee. It was a rare Scandinavian kitchen that did not always have a big pot of coffee on the back of the range and a plate of sweet pastry on the table. These kitchens were somehow different from others; maybe because they smelled so good.

Minnesota — which looked so much like the Old Country with its lakes and forests — quickly took its place as a new homeland in Swedish hearts. Like families, small towns have their "inside" jokes, and one of our town's was about a Swede who left Minneapolis to work in Chicago, fell on hard times, and announced bitterly, "To hell with United States — Aye ban go back to Minnesota."

Our town was full of Johnsons, Olsons, Swansons, Carlsons, Jorgensons, Hansons, Petersons, Nelsons, and Halvorsons. They were all newcomers in a sense, and so they tended to flock together. They had their own churches, lodges, and social organizations, and they had the Viking Chorus.[12] I never really saw the Viking Chorus, and perhaps some of its fascination lay in its incorporeity. I always imagined a circle of large men with blond mustaches around a keg of Moosehead Beer, a few playing wind instruments, the others gently waving their mugs and singing Old Country songs. At any rate, it was pleasant to sit on our porch swing of a summer evening and listen to the harmonies of the Viking Chorus wafting across town from somewhere in the darkness.

The Swedes and Norwegians acculturated rapidly, and soon they had established themselves as solid citizens, good neighbors, and staunch Republicans. With their flaxen hair and azure eyes, it might be added, some of the Swedish girls possessed a style of beauty that not even a small boy could wholly ignore.

The Finns of our town were not as well integrated as the Swedes and Norwegians, perhaps because they were later arrivals in the pecking order and spoke a language that nobody could hope to understand — except, of course, another Finn. A sizable section of Cloquet became known as Finntown. It was distinguished by a huge frame boardinghouse, a community sauna, and houses painted in vivid shades of pink, green, blue, and mauve — people called them Finlander colors.

Finnish youngsters had odd names like Toivo, Aune, Lyyli, Ilta, Reino, Unno, and Kusti, but after you had said them a few times, they somehow sounded no stranger than Albert, Donald, or Mary. They were very bright in school, good at games, and took naturally to our ways.

About the only special character trait I can recall in my Finnish agemates was a tendency to be laconic. Like Kusti Maki, for instance. Once a friend and I arranged to meet Kusti on a squirrel-hunting expedition. The rendezvous was a deserted cabin quite deep in the woods. When we arrived, no one was on hand, but there was a note on the door that read: "I have came and I have went. Kusti."

My friend, himself a Finn, thought this was rather wordy. "He didn't have to tell us he was here," he said. "We could see that!"

Your closest friend in a town like ours was likely to live in your own neighborhood. Mine was a Finnish boy named Eddie Kuitu.[13] He lived on Fourth Street, a couple of blocks away, and we devised a way of communicating with each other by means of a special recognition signal — something between a wolf howl and a yodel — that had remarkable carrying power. On a still winter morning, if I gave "the call" while carrying in wood for the kitchen stove, I would be pretty sure to hear it answered by Eddie.

We had another private call, but where it originated or

why, I do not know. Certainly it made no sense, yet we shouted it, often in unison, with the greatest enthusiasm. It went:

A Gratziano (*forte*)
And a Zipriano (*fortissimo*) — (pause)
Kee-lee (*falsetto*)

Small boys are hard to explain!

Eddie's folks had a sauna in their back yard, next to the cowshed. It wasn't much like the streamlined saunas that even city apartment dwellers boast of nowadays. Kuitus' had a rough brick firebox stoked with birch logs, and above it was a bed of smooth, round stones. When the stones became practically white hot, you threw a pail of water on them to produce steam. Then you climbed up on a tier of plank seats (the higher you climbed, the hotter it got) and gasped for breath. Next, you splashed on a little water, soaped up, and beat one another with bundles of sweet-smelling cedar twigs. Finally, you escaped to the anteroom where a couple of barrels of ice-cold water stood, emptied a bucket over your head, and yelled bloody murder.

On Saturdays the Kuitus opened their sauna to hardy friends and neighbors, charging a small fee to cover operating expenses. We kids earned our way in by carrying water for the sauna from Kuitus' pump. It is the only time I can remember having willingly worked for the privilege of taking a bath.

Ethnicity was not fashionable in those days, and I doubt that many people in our town had much appreciation of Finland's cultural riches. But somehow a copy of the great Finnish epic, the *Kalevala*, had got into the public library. One day I drew it out, along with a book on the mechanics of the steam engine (I was running out of titles). On my way home I sat under a maple tree that grew near the library and looked into the *Kalevala*. An hour later I was still lost in it — and feeling pretty bad about the lovely Aino, who had just given her life to "the deep and boundless blue sea."[14]

Hung her ribbons on the aspen,
Left her gold cross on the seashore,
Silken robes upon the alders,

On the rocks her silken stockings,
On the grass her shoes of deerskin,
In the sand her shining necklace,
In the sand her rings and jewels . . .

I was not too young to sense the beauty and nobility of the great poem, and I finished the *Kalevala* with some fresh new ideas about our townsmen the Finns.

Not a single black family lived in our town. The only Chinese was Sue Shong, the laundryman. He wore a queue and his shirt outside his trousers, and sometimes you could look through his window and see him behind his counter, eating his rice with chopsticks. He marked the shirts of his customers with Chinese characters, and there was a rumor that some of them were not altogether complimentary to the owners. It never occurred to us how lonely Sue Shong must be, but on October 20, 1906, the *Pine Knot* printed a short notice that he had killed himself in his laundry.

There were not many Germans in Cloquet, or Poles, and only a few Italians and Jews. Slightly less than half of our population was foreign born, and most of that was north European.[15] Perhaps we might have benefited from a little more southern and non-European stock — an infusion, so to speak, of warmer blood. Still, it could not be said that our town's ethnic mix was without color. And a boy could consider himself lucky, I think, to have grown up in a small place that spoke English, Swedish, Norwegian, Finnish — and even a little Chippewa.

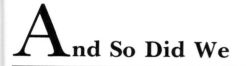And So Did We

MY FATHER, Michael O'Meara, was among the earliest of the loggers to follow the pine from the Wisconsin Chippewa River country to Minnesota. When he died in 1948, the papers spoke of him as a pioneer resident of Cloquet, and I guess he deserved the term, having lived in the town for sixty-one years, almost from its beginning.[1]

Our branch of the family migrated to America, like so many others, during the Great Hunger in Ireland. My grandfather, John, came to Canada in the 1840s, and his father, who was also named Michael, joined him later. Michael was a "hedgemaster," a schoolteacher who, at grave risk of his life, gathered the children of his village in Ireland and taught them to read and write behind the hedges or some other secret place, contrary to English law.

Most families have a legend or two, and one of ours concerned my grandfather's voyage from Ireland. He set sail for New York, it was said, but the square-rigger on which he took passage was disabled by a storm and abandoned by her crew and passengers — by all but the captain, that is, and my grandfather. The ship weathered the storm, however, and my grandfather was taken off her by a passing ship bound for Halifax. So that is how he happened to land in Canada instead of the United States.

The O'Mearas all became farmers in the province of Ontario close to a village called Ingersoll. Nearby was the infamous Roman Road, along which the Black Donnellys carried out their frightful depredations. But I trust that the O'Mearas kept clear of the "murders, gang wars, highway robbery, mass arson, derailed trains, mutilations, and barbarisms paralleling the Dark Ages" that distinguished life along the Roman Road.[2] I never heard my father so much as mention this terrifying family or the horrible old woman who was its leader. There was a vague tradition that someone in a distant branch of our sept left Canada "between two days," after burning an Orangeman's lodge. But I take that story to be apocryphal. Certainly my father and all the uncles on his side were quiet, law-abiding, mild-mannered men.

In Canada my grandfather married a North Ireland girl named Ellen Jane Carruthers. They had nine children, eight boys and finally a girl. Life was hard on the Canadian land, with little time for anything but work, and almost none for a boy's schooling. While still a young man, my father left Canada for the United States, and in the 1880s he went to Cloquet, still a backwoods village. Although he lacked learning, he was good at figures and became a scaler for the lumber companies. By laying his scaling rule across the end of a log, he could compute exactly how many board feet of lumber that log would yield. The results were entered on a large sheet of paper, and when my father came home from work, he would sometimes bring these sheets with him and add up the columns of figures. He did this with computerlike speed and accuracy, and it was always a matter of wonder to me how swiftly his pencil moved up and down the long, neat columns.

For all the rest of his life, my father remained a scaler in the mills and in the woods. An honest, hard-working, fanatically conscientious man, he lacked the education and self-centered drive that carries one to what is called "success" in life. But everyone in our town knew him as a good and honorable man.

How my mother came to live in a rough, new sawmill town, I do not know. She was not strong physically, and the rigors of life in a place like Cloquet must have been trying. But she came, nevertheless, with an older friend named Ellen Fornance (whom I shall introduce later), and opened a millinery shop.[3] Hats were important to women in those days, and they were often made to order, complete with flowers, feathers, and even stuffed birds. My mother apparently had a talent for designing and trimming these creations.

Before her marriage, my mother's name was Mary Wolfe, but everyone called her Mae. Her father, Andrew Wolfe, was a Kentuckian. I am uncertain about his background, but he may have come to America from England. His family may have migrated in quite early times; I believe there is a Wolfe County in Kentucky.

My grandmother's maiden name was Josephine Augustina Jahn. In 1846 she came to the United States from Germany at the age of three. She and Andrew Wolfe lived in Louisville, Kentucky, for a while after their marriage. They had six children, two of whom were boys named for Revolutionary War heroes, Charles Carroll of Carrollton and General Francis Marion, the Swamp Fox. The four girls were my aunts, Victoria, Rachel, and Katherine, and my mother, Mary.

Sometime before the Civil War, Andrew Wolfe and his family moved from Kentucky to Indiana, then to the Territory of Minnesota. He settled in southwestern Minnesota near the village of Montevideo, where he died in 1876 at the age of thirty-eight.[4] I often wondered how my grandmother, with six small children to care for, managed after that. From the tales she told us of prairie life in those difficult times, I am sure it took a lot of heart.

My mother must have come to Cloquet in the 1890s, since I, her first child, was born in 1897. My sister Helen arrived two years later, and Frances two years after that. My mother has been dead for half a century, and my memory of her has faded. But for some odd reason one fleeting picture of her has remained particularly vivid: a Sunday morning when, sitting beside her in church, the rose and blue lights from a stained-glass window fell on her smooth dark hair and serene face as she told her beads, and I thought how beautiful she was.

For many years, although not even distantly related to us, Dotas was a member of our family. I have already mentioned her by her true name, Ellen Fornance, as an old friend of my mother's. She was a diminutive woman, very Irish and — at least so it seemed to us children — much older than our mother. She had white hair, at any rate, which she kept neatly groomed with vaseline and adorned with a small black velvet bow. She dipped snuff and, I am afraid, tippled. She kept a case of porter in our cellar and took a good deal of Peruna, a popular tonic of the period with a high alcoholic content. When Dotas felt particularly unable to cope, she resorted to a bottle of Duffy's Pure Malt Whisky — "the Great Restorer of Youth" — with disastrous results that our mother did her best to conceal from us.

What had happened to Dotas' husband was a matter of endless speculation with my sisters and me. She had a life-size photograph of him — a melancholy-looking man with drooping mustaches — in her room. It was surrounded by a heavy gilt frame and mounted on an easel made of spools. Was he dead, we wondered, or had he simply gone away? Sometimes we doubted that he had ever existed — as Dotas' husband, that is. But we never asked about him, and Dotas did not enlighten us.

There was another mystery about Dotas. When my father was away during the winter and we wanted one of our chickens for Sunday dinner, it was Dotas who killed it. But how she did it, she would never let us know. She would simply go into the stormshed with the hen or rooster, and when she returned a few minutes later, it would be ready for plucking.

Dotas was usually gay and cheerful, with a ready store of what was called Irish wit. I am sure she did much to keep up my mother's spirits during the lonely winters with my father away in the woods. On one subject, however, she was morosely serious. When she died, she occasionally reminded us, she was not, repeat not, to be "laid out" by Mr. Moses, the local undertaker and furniture store proprietor.[5]

After living with us through most of our childhood, Dotas bought a nice little house in Minneapolis and went there to live. I have forgotten to mention still another mystery about her: she seemed to have a good deal of money invested in mortgages, and her lawyer, Mr. Fesenbeck, always treated her

My sisters Helen (left) and Frances (right) and myself at about the time covered by this meandering memoir.

My father, Michael O'Meara, proudly holding his first-born, a son who would one day write this book of memories. Photo by Johnson, Cloquet.

My grandfather, Andrew
Wolfe, who died young
and whom I never saw.

My mother, Mary Josephine
O'Meara. As a young woman
she went to Cloquet to brave life
in a small, raw sawmill town.
Photo by J. Frank Smith, Minneapolis.

My grandmother, Josephine
Augustina Wolfe, went from
Kentucky to Minnesota in a
covered wagon and saw the bad
as well as the good of pioneer
life. Photo by Thibodeau, Minneapolis.

Aunt Dell (Rachel Adell Ellery) was the romantic member of our family. She wrote poetry and painted flowers on china. Photo by D. B. Nye, Minneapolis.

Uncle Frank (Francis Marion Wolfe) brought us rare glimpses of the glamorous world of the traveling salesman. Photo by Thibodeau, Minneapolis.

Ellen Fornance, whom we called "Dotas," brought Irish wit along with a bit of the brogue and a dash of mystery to our family.

Uncle Charlie (Charles Carroll Wolfe), who had been in the navy during the Spanish-American War, was a kind of family hero. Photo by E. Nelson & Company, Minneapolis.

Aunt Vic (Victoria Philomena Howell) wore diamond solitaires in her ears and made delicious dollar-size pancakes for visiting nieces and nephew. Photo by D. B. Nye, Minneapolis.

very respectfully. But I don't believe even my mother knew the source of her wealth.[6]

Many families in Cloquet had someone living with them, relatives or otherwise, and for several years we had a pleasant, apple-cheeked farm girl named Percie Hillbrand. There was no consolidated school near Cloquet in those days, and the only way Percie could get a high school education was to move into town and live with someone as what today would be called a mother's helper. She soon became part of our family, sharing our life as an elder daughter would, helping my mother with her housework and looking after my sisters. She was a jolly but very serious girl, and I myself was overawed and a little depressed by her fierce determination to obtain an education — perhaps because it gave me, who had no great enthusiasm for school, a twinge of conscience.

After she had finished school and left us, I did not see Percie again for many years. By that time she had served and retired as elementary school supervisor for the Minnesota State Department of Education, was the author of several books, and had traveled to all parts of the world.[7]

Besides Dotas and Percie, who lived with us more or less permanently, we always had visiting relatives during the summer months. And most important of these was Grandma.

Grandma, who had gone to Minnesota in a covered wagon, never got over a chronic wanderlust. Even when she was very old — as it seemed to us — she would impulsively pack her valise and set out from St. Paul to visit one of her children or even a distant relative in some far part of the state. Once she went as far as Pittsburgh.

In her later years Grandma's mind occasionally played her tricks. When she came to visit us in Cloquet, for instance, she was apt to confuse our town with Barnum, a small whistle-stop about sixteen miles away on the Northern Pacific Railway. When this happened, the stationmaster at the depot sent up word, and there was nothing for my father to do but hire a rig at Johnson's livery stable and drive to Barnum for

Grandma.[8] Most of an anxious night might pass before he returned with her, to be greeted with relief and joy after so harrowing an experience in a strange, faraway place.

The hard, sometimes desperate life that Grandma had led on the prairies had left its mark. Her voice would sound weary and perhaps sad when she told us about the early days, when the buffalo trails ran a foot deep past their sod house. There was the terrible winter of the smallpox, when there was nobody strong enough to dig graves in the frozen ground, so that settlers had to keep their dead in their barns until spring. She told us often about the cyclones, when everybody had to scurry to the storm cellars in the field — and hope that when they came out, their house would still be standing. And most harrowing of all were her tales of the Sioux Uprising of 1862, when hundreds of settlers in the Minnesota River Valley were killed by Chief Little Crow and his warriors.[9]

So many of Grandma's memories were of hardship, and suffering, and danger. She had seen so much of the downright meanness and ugliness of pioneer life that are rarely mentioned in the schoolbook histories of our frontiers. Her face was lined with old anxieties, and her eyes were dim with a weariness that was not alone the fatigue of age.

⋀

Besides my Aunt Kate, who lived on a farm near the old family homestead in southern Minnesota, my mother had two married sisters in the Twin Cities. My Aunt Vic was the rich member of our family. She lived in a grand stone house in Minneapolis and wore big diamond solitaires as earbobs. When we visited her in the summer, she gave us delicious dollar-size pancakes with real maple syrup for breakfast. My Aunt Dell, the romantic one, lived in St. Paul. She wrote poetry, some of which was published in newspapers, embroidered beautiful vestments for her parish church, and painted china. It was Aunt Dell who kept a record of family births and deaths in my grandfather's Bible, reserving a place for her own epitaph at the end. I now own this ancient Bible, and at the bottom of the last page is written in Aunt Dell's rather florid hand, "Now the book is closed. We are all gone."

Since neither of these aunts had children of their own, they doted on my sisters and me. I guess my sisters enjoyed it, but to a small boy a lady's show of affection can be very embarrassing. I remember especially my discomfiture when Aunt Dell would tell fondly about the time (when I was very young) that I was left behind on a stroll, and called out in my childish voice, "Wait for little I'm!"

Every summer our mother took us to visit our aunts in the Twin Cities. It was an all-day train journey, so we took a big lunch of fried chicken, bread-and-butter sandwiches, chocolate cake, and bananas in a couple of shoe boxes. Oddly enough, I cannot remember very much about these excursions to the big city. I recall vaguely the aquarium in Dayton's department store (lighted under water!), the yellow, open streetcars, the floral gates ajar in St. Paul's Como Park; but better than anything else, I remember the smell of illuminating gas and the fruit stands in the railway station. They will always be "city smells" to me.

Almost every summer Aunt Dell and Aunt Vic came to visit us in Cloquet, bringing into our house a faint breath of the city. And my mother's brother Frank, who was a traveling salesman for the Crane Company, a plumbing firm, occasionally dropped by when business took him to Duluth. Uncle Frank had an air of worldly importance that seemed almost to set him apart from the rest of us; it was difficult to accept the fact that this genial gentleman, with his pearl scarfpin, fragrant cigars, and casual references to such famous hotels as the Palmer House in Chicago, was really one of our family. But if we were somewhat overawed by all this, we were nonetheless fond of Uncle Frank, especially since he always presented my mother with a large box of chocolates. When she protested, he explained that it went on something mysteriously called an "expense account."

Three teen-age cousins, daughters of my Aunt Kate — the twins Mae and Maud and their younger sister Alta — occasionally came to stay with us during the summer. They were very pretty, I thought shyly, wore their hair in extravagant pompadours, dressed in daring peekaboo waists and ankle-length skirts, and generally made the girls of our town look pretty dowdy — a circumstance, I am sure, they were not unaware of.

My cousins' vivacious chatter sparkled with smart patter that would not reach Cloquet for months, if ever; and several times I actually heard them using the words "hell" and "damn." They also brought with them the latest songs, as yet unsung in our town, like "Red Wing," "Iola," and "Honey Boy."[10] And there was one, "Coax Me, Come On and Coax Me," that (I did not understand why) my mother scolded them for singing.[11]

While my cousins were visiting us, I noted with a kind of disquiet which might have been jealousy that a remarkably large number of young men found some pretext or other for hanging around our front porch. One of the laziest of them actually offered to relieve me of my job of mowing the lawn.

Other relatives visited us at rarer intervals, among them my Uncle Charlie and Uncle Dan. We had a picture of my Uncle Charlie as a sailor on a battleship during the Spanish-American War. He became a detective on the Minneapolis police force and once he gave me a policeman's whistle, which made me the envy of the other kids. Uncle Dan was a quiet man, a bachelor, who lived farther north in Virginia, Minnesota, on the Mesabi Iron Range. For many years we all received exactly the same box of candy from him at Christmas, and we always gave him a necktie.

By far the most exciting of our uncles, however, was Uncle Will, who lived in the mountains of Idaho. He too was a bachelor, with no kin closer than ourselves. He was a tall, rangy man with glinting blue eyes under heavy eyebrows and a half-quizzical smile always playing on his weathered face. He could have stepped right into any television western, if there had been such a thing then.

Uncle Will and a partner had a copper mine somewhere in the mountains, but it was so inaccessible that he had never been able to take out more than a few loads of ore by muleback. He always brought a small sack of samples, however, for us to marvel at and display alongside some nuggets we had of native Lake Superior copper. Once he brought us a hatrack made of polished steer horns, which my mother was puzzled to find a place for. He never forgot to bring presents for all of us, and on one especially great occasion he gave me a Winchester.22-caliber repeating rifle.

Uncle Will used to enthrall us with stories about his adventures in the West — about the trips, for instance, that he and his partner would sometimes take "to see the country." On one of these trips, he said, they loaded up a couple of pack horses and started north with no special goal in mind. They continued until they came to country where mosquitoes assailed them on the snowfields and it remained light most of the night.

"How did you find your way, Uncle Will?" I remember asking him.

"We followed the mountains," Uncle Will said.

⽊

I suppose there was really nothing unusual about our family. We were just one among a thousand others in a small northern sawmill town. Yet it did not seem so to us. Like primitive tribes that have no name for themselves but "the People," because they cannot conceive of anyone else sharing their uniqueness, we felt ourselves different and special. There was something a little queer about all other families, indeed, something not quite right. How could there be a proper family, for example, without a Dotas or an Uncle Will?

I suppose all children feel this way: they find it difficult to imagine things other than as they have known them from the beginning of time. So I remember our family as I remember the other unchanging, unchangeable facts of my childhood: the deep, slow-moving river, the hills aflame with maples in September, the cloud-piled summer sky — all things that could not and never would be different. And some of this quality of uniqueness seemed to attach even to the ordinary house in which we lived.

CHAPTER FOUR

Something Over Our Heads

A MAN old enough to remember his boyhood around the turn of the century recalls the house he lived in. Not the houses — the *house*. For the one you were born in was apt to be the only home you ever knew until you left it for good.

It was where you lay in your crib and tried to figure out that rain stain on the ceiling . . . where you crawled triumphantly to the top of the stairs . . . where you chased bumblebees in the nasturtium bed . . . where you carried in wood for the cookstove and water for its "resevoy" . . . where you shoveled a path through snow over your head . . . where you did your homework under a lamp hanging over the dining-room table . . . where you said good-by at last, and never came back.

I left our house in Cloquet — the only house I really remember — in 1917, when Eddie Kuitu and I went down to Duluth to enlist in the army during World War I. When I came back, the Great Fire had destroyed the town so completely that there was no sign of our house in the ashes.[1] Yet, even at this distance in time, I remember that house better than any I have ever lived in. I remember every detail of it, right down to the small hole in the screen door and the robins' nest in the woodbine climbing up the porch.

Our house was on Third Street, on the hill that rose from the river flats. It had the high-pitched roof necessary to shed the great snows of our northern winters, twin gables, a wide front porch, a bay window on the dining-room side, a stormshed — about the standard house plan for our town. It was, of course, built entirely of wood and sheathed in the

narrow clapboards that were then considered more fashionable than the wider New England type. It was painted a warm
putty gray, with white trim.

My father hired a contractor to build our house, but he
himself did much of the interior work.[2] This took several
years, and one of our upstairs rooms never did get finished.
As soon as it was habitable, however, we moved into our new
home, and my father, who had a strong sense of fundamen-
tals, said: "Well, now we've got a roof over our heads. When
you've got something over your head and a few dollars in
your pocket, there's nothing to worry about."

Our house stood on a rather narrow but deep lot. In the
back yard there was a woodshed stacked with firewood and
a bin full of hard coal. Attached to the woodshed was a
henhouse and a small yard fenced in with chicken wire. Inside the woodshed — a rather elegant touch — was our privy.
Most people posted theirs shamelessly in the open. In the
gabled peak of the woodshed was a small birdhouse made of a
cornstarch box in which lived a couple of noisy wrens.

Our yard was like a Chinese peasant's farm; every inch of it
served some useful or aesthetic purpose. A small lawn shaded
by three or four box-elder trees flanked the house on one
side, a dirt driveway on the other. Borders of old-fashioned
flowers — nasturtiums, petunias, pansies — surrounded our
house, and a screen of sweet peas separated the back yard
from the front lawn. My mother loved flowers and was good
with them; in 1906 we won third prize in a contest sponsored
by the town for the prettiest yards in Cloquet.[3]

In our back yard were the vegetable garden and potato
patch that provided us with much of our food, summer and
winter. Here, too, were stacked the long piles of firewood
drying out before being stacked in the woodshed. And one
forgotten corner between the chicken coop and our
neighbor's fence provided me with space in which to build an
iceboat from a couple of boards, some skates, and a piece of
oilcloth; a scooter from an old baby buggy; and a glider I
never finished because I could find nothing with which to
cover it.

The front steps of our house led to a wide porch. At one side of the steps, a heavy curtain of woodbine screened the parlor window from the street and provided living quarters for a pair of robins that returned every spring to raise a family. You could lie in the porch swing and watch the whole process of domestic bird life, from building a nest to pushing the stupid fledglings out of it.

From our porch you went through the front door into a small hall with a staircase leading to the second floor. On the wall facing the door was an oval looking glass, and beside it Uncle Will's steer-horn hatrack. Near a small table under the looking glass stood an umbrella stand covered with highly varnished cigar bands, the latest craze. Since my father did not smoke, it took a good deal of begging from cigar-smoking friends and relatives to get enough bands to cover the umbrella stand.

Two doors opened from the front hall, one into the living room, the other into the parlor. The living room, which doubled as a company dining room, had a large round table that served as a center at which we all gathered to play games, do homework, write letters, cut material for dresses, wrap Christmas presents, and so on. A hanging kerosene lamp with a stained-glass shade shed a soft light over it at night.

There was a worn sofa against one wall, the old-fashioned kind that curved up and over at one end, a few straight-back chairs, and an old rocker. But what dominated the room was our Radiant Home Base Burner. It probably was not really as monumental as it seemed to a small boy, but with its bright nickel trim and many-paneled isinglass windows glowing with red-hot coals, it surely was the most impressive feature of our living room, and even of our whole house.

The other door from our front hall led to the parlor, but it was always closed. You entered our parlor through the living room, by way of a wide archway curtained with strings of eucalyptus seeds and glass beads. This curtain was brought back from California by my Aunt Vic, and it will give you an idea of what our parlor was like. It was more of a museum, really, than a place for living. We seldom entered it. Yet it was part of our house, and, now that I reflect on it, an important part. It served an instinct that was very strong in those days: a sense of family pride and self-respect that went along with shining one's shoes on Sunday morning and paying one's bills on time.

The walls of our parlor were calcimined an apple green, with tieback lace curtains at the windows and an ingrain carpet, gay with cabbage roses, on the floor. It is odd that I cannot recall the furniture very well — or perhaps not so odd, since it was seldom used. I seem to recall some golden-oak pieces and a small center table on which rested our family Bible, a massive book, at least four inches thick, with deeply embossed covers of lacquered leather held together by brass clasps. It was never opened except to record a birth on a brightly illuminated page provided for that purpose. Under the table on which the Book rested was a shelf holding a large pink conch shell of mysterious origin. By placing it to your ear, you could plainly hear the roar of the sea.

As any respectable parlor must, ours also boasted a piano. Some people, like the Fergusons, had organs in their parlors, with numerous stops and pedals, and sometimes a device that could produce a mandolin or zither effect. Our upright Baldwin could not, of course, compete with anything like that; but with its really fine Circassian walnut cabinet it was an impressive piece of furniture. A number of *objets d'art* adorned the top of our piano; the only one I can remember was a painted plaster bust of an Indian maiden, complete with war bonnet.

I was coerced by my mother into taking piano lessons, but I never progressed beyond "The Burning of Rome" and "Ben Hur's Chariot Race." I think my aversion to the piano really derived from a dislike of my music teacher. Her house was full of cats. She took in any stray that happened along and finally had to build a special house for them, with little doors through which they could go in and out. It was said that when there was no more room, she would have all the cats "put to sleep." I always went to my music lessons with dragging feet.

🌲

In one corner of our parlor stood a glassed-in bookcase with our family's small and rather oddly assorted store of

literature. My father probably had read no more than one
book, Edward Bellamy's *Looking Backward*, from which he
quoted sagely from time to time. My mother's taste inclined
toward the popular novelists, like Marie Corelli and Ouida,[4]
and she and Dotas sometimes read to each other in the evening. Occasionally, after we had finished our school work, my
mother would read to my sisters and me. She had a soft,
gentle voice, and I can recall very distinctly her reading
Robinson Crusoe.

Among the volumes in our bookcase was a coffee-table edition of Tennyson's *Idylls of the King*, illustrated with fine steel
engravings: I remember particularly a bevy of undraped
ladies cavorting on the seashore, perhaps Sir Lancelot's vision. There was also a copy of *The Farmer's Guide*, with pictures
of rectangular beef cattle and a diagram proving that it took
no more pickets to go over a hill than for a fence on level
ground. And there was a copy of Ella Wheeler Wilcox's
poems, at that time very highly esteemed. But best of all, I can
recall the works of Will Carleton, two immensely popular volumes entitled *Farm Ballads* and *City Ballads*, both glorifying
life on the farm and deploring the sins of the big city. I also
recall a poem in another book depicting the dilemma of a poor
farm couple who were about to give up one of their numerous
children to a rich relative in the City.

> Which shall it be, which shall it be?
> I looked at John and John looked at me.
> Poor patient John, who loves me yet
> As much as when my locks were jet.

I was also deeply touched by such sorrowful pieces as "Over
the Hill to the Poor-house." (Incidentally, the torn couple
above decided not to give up their child after all.)[5]

There was, of course, the "doctor book," in this case a worn
copy of *The People's Common Sense Medical Adviser in Plain
English* by the eminent R. V. Pierce, M.D. It was a book that,
the author hinted darkly, "should not be excluded from the
young, for it . . . imparts information without which millions
will suffer untold misery."[6] It certainly imparted plenty of
symptoms (fully illustrated) for a young imagination to work

on, and there were not many diseases, from coxalgia to general debility, that I did not from time to time find myself afflicted with. The book, however, offered an offsetting reassurance: no matter what the malady, if worse came to worst, a sure cure was guaranteed by a few bottles of Dr. Pierce's Golden Medical Discovery.

And now I come to the feature that really set our parlor apart from any other in our town: the genuine oil paintings that adorned its walls. These paintings were all done by Aunt Vic, who sent them to us, already framed, from Minneapolis. Aunt Vic's talents as a painter may have been limited, but her work was by no means primitive. When surrounded by an ornate gilt frame, her flower pieces and sunsets made a really impressive showing on our parlor walls. It was always a matter of special pride with us that, while other families in Cloquet had nothing but lurid "holy pictures," chromos like "The Great Chicago Fire," or perhaps a mezzotint of Rosa Bonheur's "The Horse Fair," we had the only real oil paintings in town.

It is true that our parlor was excessively formal — more like a museum, as I have said, than a room in which to live. Yet I cannot say that I remember it without respect. It was, after all, where my mother entertained company; where my sisters had their birthday parties, with chocolate in tiny Haviland cups taken from the locked china closet only on very special occasions; where our Christmas tree stood, casting a wavering light over the room; and where my mother, at last, lay in her coffin.

🌲

As in any small-town household around the turn of the century, the center of family life was our kitchen. It was a square room with painted wainscoting, large enough to accommodate the many activities that naturally went on there. And its heart was the big cast-iron cookstove that occupied most of one wall.

Like our base burner, this kitchen range was ornate with nickel trim, and scarcely a square inch of its surface lacked the sculptured swirls and fronds of botanically impossible foliage. They don't make stoves any more as beautiful as our kitchen range.

But it was also admirably functional. Its oven was capacious enough to receive the four large loaves of bread my mother baked every Tuesday and Friday. Its polished top, with six lids, could accommodate a soup pot, two skillets, a tea kettle, and wash boiler on Mondays. A "resevoy" at the back held a limitless supply of water — or so it seemed to a small boy charged with keeping it filled. A warming oven through which the stovepipe ran kept my father's supper hot while he washed up after work. And a shelf extending from the reservoir assured my mother's bread a warm, even temperature while it was rising.

Except on rare occasions when we had company, the kitchen was where we ate our meals. We sat down to supper at a big, square table covered with checkered oilcloth and lit by an ordinary glass kerosene table lamp. Some people in our town had other furniture in their kitchen, a Morris chair, perhaps, or even a couch. But besides our table and straight-back chairs, I can remember only the washstand with its basin, roller towel, mirror, and bracket kerosene lamp on the wall for light on dark evenings.

From the kitchen the back door of our house opened into a stormshed which, like a sort of air lock, stood between our house and the outside world in times of great cold or heavy weather. It was always crammed with odd pieces of furniture, a washing machine, a broken rocking chair, an outgrown rocking horse, skiis and sleds, and in deep winter a big pine chest full of frozen meat. Just off the kitchen was a pantry we shall visit later; in its floor was a trapdoor leading down to the cellar.

Our parents' sleeping quarters were on the first floor, next to the living room. The base burner was near their door, so they were quite comfortable during the coldest winter nights. The other bedrooms — three of them — were upstairs. My sisters slept in one, I in another. I guess you could say my room was furnished in rather Spartan fashion, with only a bed, chair, and small table. (However, I was better off than my friend Swipes Johnson, whose bedroom contained only a box spring and mattress on four beer kegs.) The third room on our second floor was the private apartment of Dotas, who enjoyed the luxury of a huge feather bed on winter nights. This was the one room in the house we children never entered.

🌲

When we lived downtown in "the old house," we had to carry water from a spring maintained by one of the lumber companies. I can remember, although dimly, pulling a keg to this spring on a sled encased in ice. I was not more than seven years old, but with my father "up in the woods," there was nobody else in our family to keep us in water. I was the man of the house.

When we moved uptown, no water had yet been piped into the new neighborhood. So my father made a deal with a neighbor to share his well, and it was one of my regular duties to carry our supply from this neighbor's pump. To make my work easier, my father made me a boy-size yoke from which two buckets hung. With this device and my groaning leg muscles I kept our level of water for drinking, cooking, washing clothes, and general household use reasonably adequate. At the end of each week, with a deep sense of performing unnecessary labor, I hauled an extra supply for our Saturday night baths.

It was also necessary to provide water for the Monday washdays. I do not remember the exact details of our home laundering, but I do recall clothes in a large copper-bottomed boiler on the kitchen stove, and the wash clattering on the line, stiff as sheet metal, in the wintertime. I remember, too, and not fondly, our washing machine. It was a crude wooden churn, swung back and forth by a handle. It was supposed to make washing clothes much easier than by tub and washboard; the advertisements showed a woman sitting in a rocking chair and reading a book while doing her wash. But I remember it only as an instrument of monotonous, back-breaking toil, even worse than beating rugs or shoveling snow.

For light we had kerosene lamps, and it was part of the

daily housekeeping routine to keep them filled, trim their wicks, and polish their glass chimneys. For outdoor light, we kept a lantern hanging beside the stormshed door. I often held it for my father when he was caught by failing light at some piece of carpentering or garden work. There was a special fascination about a lantern: you could swing it in circles over your head, imagining you were a brakeman on a long freight train, and the light would not go out nor the kerosene spill.

I suppose the light of a kerosene lamp was not the best to read by or sew by, but it was a mellow, friendly, somehow reassuring kind of light. There was something about touching a match to its wick, turning the little brass disk until the flame rose, and the mist inside the chimney crept slowly downward on the polished glass, that amounted almost to a rite. Irish peasants, I have heard, say a little prayer of thanks for light when they set out a lamp or candle. If you have known the daily ritual of lighting the lamps of an evening, this is something you can understand. If all you have ever done is flick a switch for light, don't even try.

So this was the house in which we lived, in which I grew to manhood. Were we happy in it? I think we were, for of all things, happiness is perhaps the most "relative." For children, the accustomed is the normal; and so, although we had few conveniences in our house, and still fewer amenities, we did not really miss what we had never known or even dreamed of. At least, I cannot remember that we complained overmuch.

CHAPTER FIVE

Digging In

MAN's first sensing of the great rhythms of nature must have come with an awareness of the seasons. It is something that people who live in cities have all but lost, something that a few trees greening in the parks, the first sooty snowfall, cannot bring back. But to those who spend their lives in the country or small towns, the year's turning is marked in a million ways, ways subtle and strident, gay and sad, gentle and sometimes cruel.

In our town the seasons were all felt deeply: the brief, violent spring; the short, hot summer; the resplendent fall; and, most of all, the long, hard winter. Even those who had to endure them made jokes about the endless Minnesota winters. So everybody appreciated the humor when "Doc," the town wag, appeared on June 21 at Moody's barbershop, pulled out his gold repeater, and after consulting it solemnly, announced: "Summer began this morning at 11:35. Winter will set in at 5:47."[1]

As a prelude to winter, our falls were short but spectacular. It was the time when the maples across the river turned almost overnight into a wall of scarlet and gold; the sky deepened from cobalt to indigo; the moon glowed blood-orange in the haze of distant forest fires; and wild geese beating southward could be heard aloft on almost any quiet night. It was the time, too, when the snowshoe hares turned white in the muskegs, boys and girls put on shoes, people gave their sleighs and cutters a coat of paint, school opened, a skim of ice formed on the milk in the pantry, and finally the millponds froze over and the mills whined to an abrupt stop. It was the time, also, of the chimney sweeps.

Every fall before the people of our town lit their winter fires, the chimney sweeps appeared briefly, then vanished into some mysterious outer world; they could not have been more fascinating if they had dropped from another planet.

There were always two of them, but whether the same two year after year no one could tell, for their faces were so masked by soot and their garb was always so much the same. They wore tall, pointed hats, like Halloween witches. On their backs they carried sooty canvas sacks containing only the tools of their trade, no doubt, their brushes, swabs, and coils of blackened rope, yet sinister-looking.

On a bright September day, the chimney sweeps might be seen atop the high-pitched roofs of Cloquet, performing their grimy rites. Sometimes they burst into snatches of wild song. Or, like a cock at dawn, one of them would pause in his work and, standing erect against the sky, raise a battered bugle to his lips. Then a shower of brassy notes would scatter over the housetops, causing women hanging out their wash to look up in surprise, dogs to bark, and children sitting near classroom windows to forget their lessons in idle dreams.

Each fall these strange men came from somewhere and advertised with song and music their alien presence among us, touching every boy and girl with some deep, perhaps atavistic longing. Ah, well, they probably weren't very efficient. The men who come today in clean coveralls with big shiny trucks and great vacuum cleaners to service your furnace do a much more thorough job, I am sure. But which of them could play a bugle from a ridgepole?

In the fall a boy naturally headed with gun in hand to the birch and poplar groves and the muskeg swamps around our town. We all owned some sort of firearm, air rifles at first, but later on "twenty-twos." My first real rifle was a .22-caliber Hamilton that I earned by selling magazines. I suppose I risked my life every time I pulled its trigger — the barrel, about eight inches long, was a strip of blued metal wrapped around a brass tube. But it seemed to me beautiful, and I cleaned and oiled it with the loving care a Kentucky frontiersman would have bestowed on his long rifle.

We hunted everything, real and imaginary, from frogs to bears. The bears never materialized, but there was always the hope one would. I am afraid that in addition to squirrels, gophers, woodchucks, and rabbits, we also shot at birds. In mitigation of this reprehensible practice, I can only say that, while blue jays, whisky-jacks, yellow hammers, and woodpeckers were considered fair play, we virtuously refrained from harming songbirds. And, to tell the truth, we seldom hit anything.

Usually a boy and one chum went hunting together, swishing along an abandoned logging road with the white birches showering down gold on their path. Sometimes the forest would echo with the rat-a-tat-tat of a redheaded woodpecker hammering on a dead pine, and we would circle stealthily, hoping to get a shot at it. Or a brace of ruffed grouse would thunder up from under our very feet and arc away through the undergrowth. Invisible red squirrels scolded, a skunk might amble across the path, or a deer start out of an alder thicket. You never knew what to expect in the woods, and even if you came home with an empty game bag — which was usually the case — there was always plenty to tell about at the supper table.

And once something happened that I did not care to tell about. Eddie Kuitu and I were hunting rabbits when we came to the edge of a clearing. The clearing sloped upward to a hill, and at the top of the hill there was a man with a rifle. He yelled to us to get back. A dog was baying in the woods surrounding the clearing, and as the baying came nearer, a deer broke into the open. The man on the hill raised his gun and fired at it. He did not hit the deer cleanly, but shattered its two front legs, and the deer got up and tried to run on the broken bones. After that time, I never cared to hunt deer.

Hunting was one of the few pleasures my father allowed himself in a lifetime of hard work. As I grew older, he would take me with him.

"Well, Walter," he would say on a Saturday evening, "shall we go and get a few birds tomorrow?"

We would get up very early, for the best time to hunt ruffed grouse — everyone called them "pa'tridges" in our town — was just at daybreak, when they were scratching in the gravel of old logging roads. After a quick breakfast, we would start out, each with his gun, ammunition, and a game bag made from a sugarsack. My father took only a few shotgun shells with him. He prided himself on getting a bird with each shell, and was quite chagrined when he failed. Before we left we would make a couple of cold meat sandwiches, and I would go down to the cellar and select two apples from our barrel of Baldwins.

We had to walk several miles in the darkness before we came to the hunting ground. It had once been a pine forest, but the timber had long since been logged off, and now there was a heavy second growth of poplar and birch. The old logging roads were still clear, however, and we would start down one of them in the half-light of the new day.

"Keep your eye skinned, Walter," my father would say.

I tried my best, but my father seemed to have sharper eyes than mine, for it was always he who stopped, slowly raised his gun, and let fly at some vague forms on the road ahead. He almost never missed, but since his old shotgun had only a single barrel, he could never get more than one in a covey of grouse. The others thundered into the trees, leaving me too surprised even to raise my gun for a futile shot at them on the wing.

At noon my father and I would sit on a log in the rustling, sweet-smelling woods and eat our sandwiches and apples. Then perhaps my father would remember how, when he was a boy in Canada, he used to hunt black squirrels in the walnut groves. He would tell me about the polished stone axes and arrowpoints he would find on his father's farm. And about the Indian boy he used to go hunting with, and how this boy could knock a squirrel out of the tallest tree with his bow and arrow. My father was away so much, and so busy about the house when he was home, that he did not have time to talk much; this was the best part of our hunting trips, really, the stories he would tell me about his boyhood.

I would not be true to the memories of my own boyhood if, in this rambling discourse, I did not at some point recall "The Shack." It had been built by Billy Horan's Uncle Harvey on his homestead beside a nameless lake about six miles north of town.[2] Since the only purpose The Shack served was to satisfy homestead requirements, Uncle Harvey seldom visited it, and he had no objection to his nephew and friends — Eddie Kuitu, Randolph Sandstrom, Carl Bruno, Don Northrup, and myself — using it as a sort of hunting and exploring base.

And so for many years, summer and winter, we made the six-mile hike through the cutover, passing a few Finnish settlers' homes at first, then following the trail, sometimes after dark, through a completely uninhabited tract. One dark night sloshing through a new snowfall something inspired us, dog-tired as we were, to compose a sort of marching song. I still remember it:

> With the gun in the hand,
>   And the pack on the back,
> And the lantern in the hand
>   For to light the track,
> It's hip! hip! hip! till we come back
> To our maws . . . to our maws.

At The Shack we had all the things a boy loves best: water, woods, freedom, companionship — and solitude. Nobody else lived near The Shack, unless you counted Joe Roy. Joe was a young Frenchman who spent an occasional day or so in his mother's homestead cabin at the far end of our lake. He was very big and strong. One evening we discerned a strange shape approaching us on the trail and, as it drew near, we made it out to be Joe with a cookstove on his back. But he was also very lazy and little inclined to make the long detour around the lake to visit us, so our solitude was seldom disturbed.

At The Shack we fished for trout in a nearby stream; set snares for rabbits on crackling winter nights and hunted them in golden autumn weather; made a canoe out of barrel hoops and a piece of canvas and paddled about in it naked as jay birds (in case it turned over); regaled ourselves on fried rabbit, baked beans, and hashed potatoes; happily explored the surrounding country without ever finding anything remarkable; or merely loafed, talked, argued about batting averages, and listened to the chickadees in the bush.

The last time I visited Cloquet, Eddie Kuitu and Carl Bruno and I — three old men — made a sort of sentimental journey to The Shack. By automobile we could not get very close to where it had once stood — there was no road. But we managed to reach the lake — it was still full of water lilies — and we stood looking across the water to where The Shack had been. We stood there for a long time, looking, and none of us could think of much to say. But then we didn't have to.

Autumn, of course, was the football season, and up until Thanksgiving our interest in the game ran high. We followed the Big Ten and Ivy League schedules avidly. We had long discussions about the forward pass, which was introduced in 1906.[3] And each fall we awaited eagerly the outcome of the annual football classic, the Yale-Harvard Thanksgiving Day game. But I cannot recall that we ourselves played much football. This was partly because the game greatly resembled mayhem in those days, and our parents forbade us to go and get our necks broken. But mostly it was because nobody in our neighborhood owned a football.

In the cool autumn months several other sports of a more or less strenuous nature became popular. One of these was shinny. Shinny was a game something like hockey played with a tin can and sticks, any sort of sticks, from broom handles to baseball bats. We often played it at night, under the sputtering carbon-arc light at a street intersection. It was accompanied by cries of "Shinny on your own side," and sometimes by the anguished yowls of a player struck on the shin by an opponent's misdirected swing at the can. The frequency with which this happened, I assume, gave the game its name.

It was during the brisk days of autumn also that we took to such grueling pastimes as wrestling and boxing. Wrestling was a clean and popular sport at that time, with Frank Gotch, George Hackenschmidt, and Strangler Lewis as well known as Joe Namath and Vida Blue are today.[4] So we wrestled a lot, practicing on one another such excruciating holds as the half nelson, hammer lock, and scissors until one contestant squawked "Uncle!" or collapsed flat on his back. It was a form of sport not much favored by mothers confronted with the Monday wash.

Even more popular than wrestling was boxing, for this was the golden age of fisticuffs, with such greats as Battling Nelson, Joe Gans, Tommy Murphy, Billy "Honey" Mellody, Kid Herman, and Jack Johnson fighting more or less honestly in towns all the way from New York to Goldfield, Nevada. Back-yard boxing in our neighborhood strove to emulate the historic ring encounters, but suffered from a want of gloves. We did the best we could with our fathers' mittens stuffed with rags, but it wasn't easy to imagine yourself a Bat Nelson or Kid Herman with a pair of striped woolen mittens dangling at the end of your lethal jabs. So we yearned powerfully for a set of real boxing gloves, and finally Billy Horan's goat was the means of our getting one.

It is easy for a small boy to develop a fixed idea about something he wants. Billy wanted a goat. Goats were advertised for sale in small-town magazines, and Billy pored over these ads and importuned his mother to buy him one. I think he dreamed of hitching it to his express wagon and driving around town as the envy of his friends.

For a long time Mrs. Horan successfully resisted the goat idea, but at last she must have sensed her defenses crumbling. Because when Billy's birthday came around and — under considerable neighborhood pressure — he began to beg for some boxing gloves, she was quick to promise him some if he would just forget about the goat.

Billy's gloves immediately became community property, of course, and the whole neighborhood resounded with the thuds and grunts of what Theodore Roosevelt had popularized as the manly art of self defense. Boxing was supposed to develop physical fitness and demonstrate the virtues of fair play and good sportsmanship, but all it ever demonstrated in our case was that Marv Pollard, a relatively new boy in the neighborhood, could whup the tar out of all the rest of us.

⅄

Toward the end of September an event occurred that, from the standpoint of a small boy, was about the only negative thing one could say about our splendid Minnesota autumn: school opened.

There must be some Freudian reason why, of all my boyhood memories, I seem to recall least vividly what went on in school. My recollections are like those patches of earth one glimpses through scattered clouds from an airplane, fleeting and hazy.

I do not, for example, remember any of my grade school teachers except Miss Tillie Mumpy, who taught second grade in the old red brick Washington School. She was a tiny woman, not at all young or good-looking, whom everyone, even kids, loved. She taught us how to create a row of cats sitting on a rail by pasting pussy willow catkins to a drawing of a fence, adding tails and heads with faces and whiskers. And I am sure she imparted a lot of other equally valuable knowledge.

Around my other teachers — all vague, wraithlike creatures — I am afraid no such memories cluster. We did not resort to direct action in those days, but a universal sentiment was no doubt expressed in a bit of doggerel we sang, or rather shouted, on the first joyous day of summer vacation:

> No more lessons,
>   No more books,
> No more teachers'
>   Ugly looks.

I would not be surprised if children still sang this uncomplimentary verse; their oral graffiti, like their stupid jokes and riddles, seem never to change.

In the fall of 1905 when we moved to our new house on Third Street, I was transferred to another school and thrown in with a lot of kids I had never seen before. One might think that in a town no larger than ours everyone, including youngsters, would know everyone else. But this was far from the case. Moving into a new neighborhood and to a new school was not unlike moving to a foreign — probably hostile — country.

The kids at my new school did not exactly welcome me to their midst. In fact, they immediately arranged a test of fisticuffs with one of their lot — a ritual procedure, I discovered later, that was standard practice whenever a new boy showed his face on the school playground.

The battle took place at the noon hour, and the boy chosen to oppose me was named Johnny Gorham. As I started for home (we always went home for lunch), this Johnny Gorham planted himself in my path.

"Who are you?" he asked, and I sensed it was anything but a polite inquiry. "What's your name?"

"Who wants to know?" I answered.

"I do."

"Well, that's too bad."

I tried to go around him, and he moved sideways to block my way.

"Where do you think you're going?"

"That's my business."

During this sparkling repartee, a crowd of boys was gathering. It closed in, and suddenly one of the boys gave me a push from behind, and the fight was on. I do not recall who won, so it was probably Johnny. Anyhow we became good friends afterward and fought no more.

I cannot even remember the name of my new school. It was, indeed, hardly worthy of being called, like other schools, after a great man such as Washington or Jefferson. It was a large, square, drab two-story building of wood, with staring four-paned windows and a bare, wind-swept yard. On one corner it had a low belfry in which the school bell hung. Kids who were relatively well behaved got to ring the bell by pulling on a rope. I cannot recall that I ever rang it.

Our classrooms probably did not differ much from those of the proverbial little red schoolhouse. Double seats had just given way to single desks, but some of the old style with twin inkwells remained in the basement, and we thought how old-fashioned they looked. Blackboards ran around two sides of the room, and teacher sat up front in a walking skirt, shirt-waist, and probably a Psyche-knot hairdo.

In the lower grades pupils still wrote their lessons on slates with pencils also made of slate that were very fragile and always breaking. Erasures were made by means of a small sponge on a string and a little spit. In the higher grades we bought tablets of rough ruled paper at least two inches thick on which to do our homework. On their red covers was printed in large type, "ALL YOU CAN CARRY 5¢." And this, with our textbooks, comprised most of our learning equipment.

Teaching had not progressed very far beyond the three R's. I am not sure that we actually used McGuffey's *Readers,* but when I examined a set of them recently, it was with a distinct sense of *déjà vu.* Learning to write consisted of endless repetitions of Spencerian letters and exercises — resulting in some-thing that looked like coiled springs — supposed to promote a flowing hand. As for arithmetic, it was still concerned largely with the problems of Harry and Tom, who never seemed to know how they would come out in swapping apples for oranges, and with Farmer Jones's profit from selling his sheep and buying cows.

In ways not much different from today's, we observed all the holidays. We cut out paper hatchets and cherries on Washington's birthday, jack-o-lanterns for Halloween, tur-keys for Thanksgiving, and pasted them on blackboards and windows just as children still do. On Valentine's Day we had a box into which boys and girls dropped valentines, and there was always a little girl who got a great many, and some who received very few or perhaps none at all — except what they had sent to themselves. Boys shyly sent pretty, unsigned val-entines to their secret loves and crude insults, called comic valentines, to other boys. We did all the usual things that are still done, for although times and schools may change, it seems that kids never do.

Once a year most parents invited their children's teachers to dinner. Since teacher was usually from out of town and considered highly educated and cultured besides, a special effort was made to provide entertainment worthy of her distinguished status. My own mother — and I suppose most others — always had the standard "company" dinner of fricasseed chicken, mashed potatoes and gravy, peas, fresh rolls, relishes, and an angel cake for dessert.

It seemed to give my mother great pleasure to entertain teacher, but for me these visits were occasions of acute embarrassment. If you happened to be on something less than warm, friendly terms with your teacher, what then? You could only observe her warily across the table, hoping that she would not carelessly let drop any secrets about your classroom behavior. You could never tell about a teacher, and it was always with a sigh of relief that you heard the front door close after her.

Of the autumn holidays, Thanksgiving was observed much as it is today: it seems to be the most unchanging of our great days — except, perhaps, for the intrusion of televised parades into the observance of a simple American festival.

Halloween, however, was kept in a manner that has all but disappeared from our folkways. We did no trick-or-treating on Halloween; we simply terrorized the good people of Cloquet without quarter. One of our instruments of terror was the ticktack. To make a ticktack you cut teeth in a spool, wound a long string around it, and stuck a tenpenny nail through the hole. When the ticktack was placed against a neighbor's window and the string jerked violently, the revolving spool produced a racket which suggested that the house was falling apart — or so, at least, we believed. Peashooters gave almost equally disturbing results. A peashooter was a metal tube through which you blew a shower of dried peas against a window. And, of course, there was the business of ringing doorbells and scurrying away before they could be answered. I cannot remember that we dressed up fancy in performing any of these nefarious rites.

Older boys engaged in less innocent forms of mischief, such as soaping windows, carrying off gates, and tipping over outhouses. They also tipped over woodpiles; I can still feel my disgust and depression when, one morning after Halloween, I found the wood I had so neatly piled all summer long scattered over our back yard.

At about the time the maples turned in the fall, a striking seasonal change also occurred in what a boy wore. If I cannot remember our summer attire very well, it is probably because there was so little of it. We often wore loose bib overalls, I believe, with many pockets — the kind carpenters and mechanics still wear. If anything at all adorned our heads during the summer, it was apt to be a house painter's cap made of a thin white material, with a shiny cardboard visor, and "JOS. LOISEL — PAINTS AND HARDWARE" printed across the front. There was a run on these caps the day the news got around that Joe was giving them away, and the whole town suddenly became a boy-and-cap advertisement for Loisel's Hardware Store.[5]

But autumnal frosts, and especially the demands of decorum that attended the opening of school, brought this idyllic mode of dress to an abrupt end. Now a boy was forced to wear — at least on school days — a knee-pants suit, a shirt, shoes and stockings, and sometimes, if his powers of resistance were low, even a necktie. When his parents bought such an outfit for him, B. J. Summerfield threw in the necktie or a pair of suspenders. And well he might; a complete set of "good clothes" could set your father back as much as $12 or $15.[6]

Kids, it seems to me, were not very fashion conscious in those days. A boy accepted whatever his parents' economic means and sartorial tastes dictated. Jo-jo Paul Joseph, the biggest and toughest kid on our street, sometimes appeared in his grown-up sister's high shoes, and nobody ever jibed at them. Not in Jo-jo's hearing, anyhow.

Whatever fashions there were changed very slowly. The only real innovation I can recall was the introduction of knickerbockers. Short pants had always been of a conservative straight-cut pattern, reaching snugly to just below the knee and adorned by a row of small buttons such as are still to be found in equally useless array on men's coat sleeves. Then knickers appeared suddenly and, while considered sissy by some of us, quickly won general acceptance. There was only one boy in Cloquet who held out against them. Sam Chapados manfully resisted the new mode, and before long became a quaint figure in his old-fashioned straight pants.

The change-over from knee pants to long trousers, on the other hand, was a momentous step in a boy's life. And, strange to say, one of no little embarrassment. It was no casual matter as it is today when moppets begin wearing long pants before they can toddle; it was a sort of putting away of the pants of a child that amounted almost to a puberty rite. I can still feel the painful self-consciousness with which I shambled to the blackboard in the eighth grade, wearing before the whole class my first long-pants suit, complete with vest.

Appearing at school in a new pair of shoes was also a serious matter. It often subjected the wearer to a somewhat inelegant hazing rite (the idea, if you must know, was to "baptize" the new shoes by spitting on them). On one such occasion, I was unfortunate enough to bash the head of one of my hazers, a boy named Earl McGilvray, against the wall of the school. McGilvray only feigned unconsciousness, of course, but so realistically that the school principal turned pale and, after ascertaining that McGilvray was still alive, suspended me from school for the rest of the day. My mother was not sympathetic. She set me to spreading manure on the potato patch, but I was thankful I had not been thrown into jail for murder. McGilvray *had* looked pretty dead.[7]

🌲

The brief, brilliant days of autumn passed swiftly, and the householder in Cloquet must waste no time in setting up his defenses against winter. Fall was a time of "digging in," of putting up storm doors and windows, cleaning flues and chimneys, stuffing the woodshed to its roof, laying in a supply of coal, and stocking the cellar with food enough to last until the return of spring.

Our back-yard garden supplied us with all the fresh vegetables and salad greens anyone could ask during the summer months, but it must also provide enough root vegetables — potatoes, carrots, beets, turnips — to fill our cellar with food for the winter. That cellar was our bastion against want and hunger. It was designed solely for the storage of food, a small, always cool room, perhaps not more than ten feet square, with thick concrete walls and one small window to let in a bit of dim, cobwebby light.

Along one wall under the steep stairs leading down from the pantry, a bin held our potato harvest. I had helped my father plant the potatoes and had tended them all summer, hilling them up, picking potato bugs and dropping them into a can of kerosene; as a kind of reward, I had been allowed to dig some of them in the fall. It was fascinating to see your fork turn up a batch of potatoes, a kind of miraculous multiplication of the small pieces dropped into the earth a few months before.

Against another wall shallower bins held carrots, beets, and turnips, snugly bedded in layers of clean sand. There would be a bushel basket or two of cabbages in one corner, a big stone crock of eggs in water glass, perhaps a keg of homemade sauerkraut and another of *lutefisk*, a Scandinavian delicacy I shall describe later. And every fall my father would buy two barrels of apples, one of Baldwins — an excellent variety seldom met with nowadays — and one of Winesaps, and the good smells of our cellar were dominated by their fragrance. Since they must last through the winter, our apple store was strictly rationed. Each evening after supper, I and my sisters selected one apiece, searching the barrel, of course, for the choicest. As a result, the quality of our apples deteriorated markedly toward spring.

A wide ledge held the rows of Mason jars and glasses of canned fruits, vegetables, pickles, and wild berries my mother had "put up" for the winter. I do not recall that we bought much for the purpose of canning, except a bushel of peaches, perhaps, and a few baskets of Concord grapes for jelly. Everything else was either grown in our own garden or — like blueberries and raspberries — gathered in the cutover timberland that encircled our town.

Of all my boyhood memories, that of our cellar remains one of the clearest, most detailed, and most pleasant. And I recall with special fondness the time I went with my father — just before he left for the woods — to take a last look around it. Slowly, as if savoring each item, my father's eyes inventoried our winter larder, the bins of vegetables, the barrels of apples, my mother's jars of fruits and "sauces," a few bottles of dandelion wine gleaming softly amber in the light of the small snowy window under the ceiling. The little, close-packed room filled the eye with the sight and gratified the nose with the sweet, damp fragrance of the earth and things of the earth. It filled the soul, too, with a comforting assurance of plenty and security, proof against the long, cold months ahead.

Above ground on that day an early December blizzard with below-zero gales howled around the house. My father cocked his ear to it and smiled; and I knew he was more than half in earnest when he said, "Well, anyhow, we can make it through the winter."

CHAPTER SIX

The Snows Came

WINTER was apt to arrive suddenly and dramatically in Cloquet. A boy might go to bed at night under a bare roof and wake up next morning to find the whole world buried in great drifts of snow.

Sometimes the snow would fall quietly for days, like a gentle white rain, covering the earth with marble contours and azure shadows. In late January it would often roar down on icy north winds that drove fiercely across roofs and piled up in sculptured, sharp-edged drifts. Still later the snows that fell in February melted quickly, edging the eaves of houses with icicles as thick as a man's leg and reaching from roof to ground. Each snow throughout the long winter fell one on top of the other, until the paths we shoveled to the woodshed were almost like tunnels, so far were their sides above a boy's head. The town's snowplows drawn by four horses could scarcely force their way along the streets.

With winter came cold that made the ice on the St. Louis River roar, caused our house to crack alarmingly at night, and drove the red thread in our thermometer down to the zero mark for a month at a time. Forty below zero was not considered unusual.

During such periods of extreme cold, parhelia (we called them sun dogs) appeared in the sky, and little white birds, known to us as "snowflakes," came down from the still colder arctic regions.[1] As many as a hundred of these snowy little creatures would gather in our yard and scratch in the wind-swept ground for seeds. My mother would strew some of the chicken feed on bare spots for them.

And now, to life under our roof was suddenly added the elemental problem of keeping warm. We battened down the storm windows, banked the house with snow, hung the storm doors, and fired up the big base burner in our living room. Our Radiant Home Base Burner had many of the virtues of an open fireplace. The whole family tended to gather around it on a frosty winter evening. You could put your stockinged feet, damp from tramping in the snow, on the nickel fenders and absorb the heat that did indeed radiate from the glowing

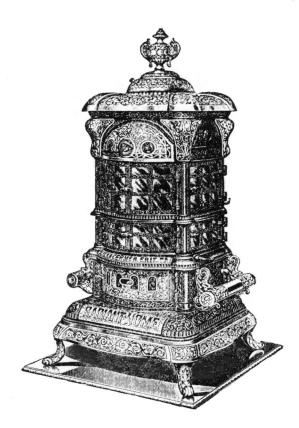

Here in all its glory is the Radiant Home Base Burner that graced our living room and around which the family gathered on a winter evening. This advertisement appeared in the Pine Knot, *October 8, 1904.*

interior. You could open the isinglass windows and roast apples on the coals. You could slide back the ornate finial at the summit and heat a kettle for tea or chocolate. And there was a little shelf in back on which a pot of beans often baked cosily. Our Radiant Home Base Burner gave off a rosy light as well as warmth, and good cheer, and a feeling of security on dark winter nights with maybe a norther beating against the windows.

Our only other means of heating was the kitchen range. On a winter day, with the mercury forty-odd degrees below zero, our kitchen was the warmest and friendliest room in the house. You could sit there and hear the crackle of the fire and the burning billets falling to ashes in the firebox. You could hear the teakettle humming, feel the flow of heat across the room, maybe catch a whiff of molasses cookies baking in the oven. With powder snow whipping around the corners and the whole world outside cracking with frost, our kitchen was not the worst of places in which to do your homework or fashion rabbit snares.

Not as much, however, could be said for our upstairs sleeping quarters. A little heat from downstairs may have seeped up, but at night there was precious little difference in temperature between our bedrooms and the arctic cold outside. Nobody but Dotas in her deep feather bed was really warm on a bitter January night. Even our chickens in their feathers, we suspected, were better off than we.

Having no running water, we were without flush toilets or bathtubs. The Saturday night bath was joke material only for city folks with hot and cold water on tap. For country people like ourselves, who had to carry the water bucket by bucket, heat it on the kitchen range, then bathe in a tin washtub on the floor — as near the stove as possible — bathing on a subzero Saturday night was not all that funny.

Even less amusing was the lack of an indoor toilet. Our privy was, as I have said, in a corner of the woodshed. This afforded some protection from freezing winds, but none against the cold itself. Even when you were young and warm-blooded, our outhouse was no place to linger over the pages of the Sears, Roebuck catalog, which — and not just in the joke books — served the purpose of toilet paper. Indeed, a trip to the privy on a black winter night came under the unsmiling classification of genuine hardship.

🌲

To combat the unrelenting cold of Minnesota winters, special clothing was required. Our first line of defense was the long woolen union suit — not just one, but two worn concurrently. Over these we donned woolen stockings, woolen pants (with suspenders), and a flannel shirt. Sometimes we wore two shirts, one over the other. One boy in our town aroused a good deal of envy in the rest of us by wearing three shirts to school, each a different color. Whether you wore one shirt or several, it was considered *de rigueur* to turn up the collars.

We protected our fingers against the frost with heavy horsehide mittens with knitted wrists. Although they were woollined, we sometimes added another pair of light woolen mittens inside for extra warmth. When you were very young, a string was attached to your mittens and passed through your sleeves around your neck to guard against loss. It was a sign of growing up when your mittens no longer dangled at the end of a string.

Much of our winter clothing was patterned after the gear of loggers. We had two kinds of winter coats; one was cut from heavy woolen material in standard plaid designs, belted at the waist, and called a Mackinaw. The other, worn by those boys whose parents could afford it, was made of sheepskin, with the fleece inside. Since it was convenient to wipe one's nose on one's sleeve instead of fishing for a handkerchief under layers of clothing, the sleeves of a boy's sheepskin coat acquired a dark, shiny patina by winter's end.

Another cold weather precaution was a knitted article called a chest protector. It fastened around the neck and looked like a turtle-neck sweater from the front, with a sort of bib over the chest. It was a favorite with parents, but older boys disdained it. As for sweaters, surprisingly enough in such a cold climate, they were not much worn. The only ones I can recall were of the heavy pull-over type. After a little wear the turtle-neck stretched, opening like the calyx of a flower with a boy's head projecting from it like the stamen.

Some of our winter days were so cold that your ears could freeze to a dead, marblelike whiteness after only a few minutes of exposure, and you would not know about it unless someone told you. So protective headgear was an absolute necessity. It was sometimes provided by a heavy stocking cap pulled down over the ears. But more common was a visored cap of woolen cloth with fur-lined earflaps (always called earlaps). We became so accustomed to these earlaps during the long winter that when spring finally arrived, we were as addicted to them as a moppet to his security blanket and wore them lowered well into the warm spring weather. Some kids never retracted them all summer.

Our winter footgear was, now that I think of it, somewhat on the unusual side. In deep winter when the temperature never rose above freezing and there was no danger of dampness, we attended school in a version of the Indian moccasin. These moccasins were made of tanned moosehide, with large brass eyelets through which leather thongs passed to lace six inches or so above the ankle. When it was really cold — say forty-eight degrees below zero — we wore as many as three pairs of thick woolen socks inside our moccasins, and a schoolroom full of pupils thus shod was not particularly sweet smelling.

We also wore a kind of boot called a shoepack. It was built of heavier, oil-tanned leather, and was quite waterproof if treated occasionally with neats-foot oil. The shoepack's distinctive feature was a pointed, turned-up toe, reminiscent of a Laplander's caribou boot. Later, when vulcanized rubber came into general use, rubber boots with leather uppers were worn by loggers, and clothing stores carried smaller sizes for boys. They, too, were worn with heavy socks and sheepskin insoles. Old-timers, accustomed to the classic Chippewa boot of the logger, sometimes complained that rubber boots did not allow the feet to "breathe."

🌲

So, in one way or another, we made shift to combat the frost and keep our houses and ourselves warm. But we also had to eat, and despite the bounty of our cellar, there was the problem of maintaining a meat supply through the long winter.

This was solved by means of our meat chest. Each year just before he left for the woods, my father would buy half a hog and a quarter of beef from Fred Grunig, the butcher.[2] Fred would cut them into steaks, chops, roasts, and stew meat; then my father stowed them in a great pine chest in our stormshed. Next morning it would all be frozen as hard as chunks of Minnesota granite, and we would have a supply of "quick-frozen" meat until spring. Of course, this freezing process required a night of intense cold, but there was seldom any lack of that in December. Our only worry was the potential disaster of an early January thaw.

For fish we depended on a farmer named Johnny White.[3] During the summer he sold vegetables from a horse-drawn wagon with a parasol over the seat to protect from the sun his old mother, who always rode with him. In winter he peddled frozen Lake Superior herring from a light sleigh, with his mother, who was very ancient and tiny, still beside him, although so bundled in robes and shawls that it was hard to make her out as a person.

When Johnny pulled up in front of our house, we ran out with a gunny sack, and for fifty cents he would fill it. The fish, sometimes called ciscoes, were caught in the cold waters off the north shore of Lake Superior. They were about the size of a brook trout with almost the same, fine textured meat, and I remember them as very good to eat. Frozen hard as sash weights, a sack full would last us through a good many winter Fridays.

In December my mother would also put up a keg of *lutefisk,* a practice she had acquired from our Swedish neighbors. We bought the *lutefisk* in the form of split stockfish, dry and hard as a hickory plank. It had to be soaked for days in lye water, which softened it and gave to some parts a kind of gelatinous character. Steamed and served with butter and boiled potatoes, it was considered by the Swedes a traditional Christmas delicacy, but I could never understand why.

Milk we obtained from a neighbor who had a cow. Every evening I would go to this neighbor with a two-quart tin pail, and the "milk lady" would fill it from a large can in her kitchen. If my mother happened to need cream for something she was making, she would pour the milk into shallow pans. By morning a yellow layer of cream had formed on the milk, and she would skim it off.

On the whole, I think our diet, supplemented by butter, eggs, and good cheese cut from a huge "wheel" at the Company Store, pretty well met the protein requirements of modern dietetics. It was in the department of fresh fruits and vegetables that difficulties obtained; sometimes I wonder why we did not all contract scurvy or beriberi during the long winters in which for six months not a single leafy vegetable or glass of orange juice appeared on our table. It may have been that the Company Store carried salad greens, lettuce and such, during the winter, and that the rich people on Chestnut Hill enjoyed them the year around. I do not know, but I do not remember that we ever bought so much as a head of lettuce.

Nor were we much better off for fresh fruit. Except for the two barrels of apples in the cellar, we had practically none from summer to summer. Oranges were unknown to us except at Christmas, when a few were hung on the Christmas tree and one was dropped into each stocking. Grapefruit, that curious mutation, was just coming to market and was suspected of being poisonous, but that was not one of our worries since none of us had ever tasted grapefruit. Except for lemons, our sources of vitamin C (which was also unknown) were few indeed.[4]

As the end of winter drew near, my mother began to crave for "greens." The first plants to appear after the snow had melted were dandelions, and as soon as they poked out of the ground she sent me with a basket and kitchen knife to gather some. While still very young and tender, they made excellent pot greens, served with a little butter, vinegar, or bacon drippings; or they could even be eaten uncooked as a green salad. Another early wild plant we called "pigweed" (more properly, and more appetizingly, known as lambs-quarters) was also cooked as a pot green. For a real salad, however, we had to wait until the lettuce in our garden came into leaf.

Yet despite all these dietary deficiencies and peculiarities, we throve. Perhaps it was because our food was at least natural, unadulterated, and unprocessed. Most of it was organically grown in our own soil with nonchemical fertilizers — we had never heard of any other — and eaten fresh from the garden in summer. If it was sometimes a little short of vitamins, it was, at any rate, free of preservatives, conditioners, and flavor enhancers.

I must add that we supplemented our "garden-and-cellar" diet with items purchased at the Company Store and Fred Grunig's meat market. But it was so seldom we visited the Company Store that I have only two dim, and rather singular, memories of it. One is of the kerosene pump in the back room. The other is of a group of laughing young ladies, clerks or customers, one of whom sang a popular song:

> Oh, please don't tell her
> I have a feller,
> Or she won't buy me
> A rubber dolly.[5]

From the Company Store we bought such staples as flour, bacon and cheese, butter in stone crocks, bagged salt, coffee and tea, lard, baking powder and soda, corn meal and oatmeal; and occasional luxuries such as sardines, cocoa, and olives. When my father paid his bill at the end of the month, we children received a paper bag of mixed candy.

Fred Grunig, who wore a straw hat in his butcher shop summer and winter, supplied us with meat — with liver, as I remember, free to anyone who cared for it. He also dispensed a little lagniappe at bill-paying time, usually a Bologna sausage, with a wiener (consumed on the spot) for any youngsters who just happened to be around. I remember particularly that we always bought a three-pound pork roast for Sunday dinner from Fred.

A mother in those days prepared food for her family "from scratch." I cannot remember anything that came into our kitchen precooked, premixed, or "instant." We ground our coffee in a little mill, cooked our oatmeal all night on the back of the stove, made our own pot cheese, bottled our own root beer, canned our own fruit and vegetables, and, of course, my mother baked all of our bread and pastries.

Flour was our big "store-boughten" item. It came in ninety-nine-pound bags (I could never understand why not a hundred pounds) and was emptied into a bin under the pantry counter. The muslin bags were saved for dishcloths. Some people even made summer underwear from them after bleaching out the trademark, and a young lady's drawers might carry a faint reminder of Pillsbury's Best or Gold Medal Flour.

Winter was naturally the time of greatest baking activity, and we had a constant supply of home-baked bread and rolls, fresh from the oven. There was always a pan of dough, it seems to me, covered with a clean dishcloth on the shelf behind the stove, or being punched down on a floured board, or emerging hot and fragrant from the oven. We hardly waited for the bread to cool before cutting it in thick slices and spreading them with butter, jam, corn syrup, or brown sugar.

Cinnamon rolls of a kind you rarely see anymore — two inches high, buttery, sticky, and studded with currants — came out of my mother's oven, too, filling the kitchen with the most heavenly smell that ever greeted a hungry small boy home from school. Of pies, we had those made from native wild berries, blueberry and raspberry; apple, of course, and rhubarb (which we called pieplant); lemon meringue, and pumpkin in the fall.

My mother baked all sorts of cakes, from gingerbread to angel food, and I shall not attempt to describe them. But one of her recipes in her own handwriting may still be found between the pages of the family Bible, and my granddaughter Nora recently baked a cake for me, using this recipe. Even allowing for a margin of nostalgia, I thought it was a great success, and so I herewith pass on to you my mother's recipe for chocolate cake. It will be noted that only ingredients and measurements are given in this recipe. It was taken for granted that any cook worth her salt knew how to combine the materials.

CHOCOLATE CAKE

1½ cups of sugar
½ cup butter
1 cup sour milk
2 eggs
½ cup hot water poured on 2 squares
of chocolate until like cream
1 teaspoon soda
2 cups flour
Bake in layers or loaf and ice with
bittersweet chocolate frosting.

Of my mother's desserts, I remember two particularly. One she learned from her Swedish friends, and I do not know the name of it. She made it by dipping a pierced iron mold, star-shaped or in the form of a rosette, in sweet batter, then plunging it into a kettle of hot fat. The confection thus produced had paper-thin walls in an intricate design; when sprinkled with powdered sugar, it looked like a big, beautiful snowflake. The second one I remember — rice pudding — is possibly the most pedestrian of all desserts, but I swear my mother's was different. She put the boiled rice through a strainer until it was just short of creamy, then folded sweetened, vanilla-flavored whipped cream into it, and served it in a sherbet glass with a dab of raspberry jam on top.

On rare occasions we made ice cream, always a complicated event of great importance. First there was the business of obtaining an extra supply of milk from the "milk lady," and setting pans of it in the pantry to gather a thick layer of cream. Then my mother prepared the custard with fresh eggs, milk, sugar, and whatever flavoring went into the fragrant yellow mixture. Finally, on the morning the ice cream was to be made, we kept a sharp lookout for Mr. Fagin.

For those families that had iceboxes, Mr. Fagin delivered blocks of ice from an enclosed wagon drawn by a single horse.

There were always chips of ice lying on the dripping tail gate of Mr. Fagin's wagon, and he never objected to our helping ourselves to them. It was refreshing to let a piece of ice melt in your mouth, but not very satisfying. I doubt that today's consumers of Popsicles — which had not yet been invented — would have considered the reward for chasing Mr. Fagin's wagon half a block worth the effort on a hot day.

On ice-cream day a dime's worth of ice was purchased from Mr. Fagin, wrapped in a piece of burlap, and stowed in a metal washtub until needed. We had a sort of toothed scoop for shaving the ice. When enough had been prepared, we packed it with alternate layers of rock salt around the shining metal cylinder in the center of the freezer. Then my mother poured in the mixture of custard and cream, inserted the three-bladed wooden paddle, and handed the job of turning the crank over to me. At first this was easy, but as the mixture began to freeze, it became more and more difficult, until at last (with my sisters urging me on) I struggled to give the handle one more turn. When I finally had to admit defeat, my mother judged the ice cream frozen. Carefully opening the freezer, she drew out the paddles (which we clamored to "lick"), and there in beautiful yellow swirls, exuding a heavenly fragrance of cream and vanilla, was what would have been called ambrosia had the gods only possessed a freezer.

Anything as special as my mother's ice cream — and so complicated in the making — had to be a feature of rare and important occasions, such as birthdays. It happened that we made it to celebrate my sister Frances' first birthday, and it became a tradition to have ice cream on each of her birthdays thereafter. It is a tradition I still observe, even though Frances has long been dead and ice cream is no longer the rare treat it was when we were all young together.

⛄

My mother's kitchen was always astir with activity or evidence of some project peripheral to the daily routine of preparing meals and baking. There would be a golden sheet of noodles drying on a clean dish towel over the back of a chair.

Or a small keg of shredded cabbage turning to sauerkraut in a warm corner. Or a bag of cottage cheese dripping whey into a pan. Perhaps even a crock of dandelion wine fermenting for the enjoyment of my father's friends, although he never drank any of it himself.

On almost any winter day after school my sisters might be found making fudge or taffy, for, except at Christmas time, most of our candy was also home-produced. Now and then, but not very often, we invested as much as a nickel in penny candy at Pat Ronan's store.[6] For one cent you could get not only such staples as jawbreakers, all-day suckers (now called lollipops), and licorice whips, but also candy eggs in little tin frying pans, sugar jugs coated with chocolate and containing a sweetish liquid we imagined to be somehow illicit, tiny sugar hearts with messages like "I love you" written on them, and many other esoteric confections that could hardly be manufactured at home. There was one very delicious nougat bar called "Old Hickory" that cost a whole nickel, but I cannot remember ever putting out that much money for a single piece of candy.

Besides foods, our kitchen produced many other things, such as medicines with which to treat winter ailments. These included: cough syrup made by boiling cedar twigs with sugar; a revolting "tonic" made by mixing molasses and flowers of sulfur; rock-and-rye, a not unpleasant concoction of rye whisky and crystals of rock candy; mustard plasters for almost all aches and pains, but especially those in the chest and back; goose (or chicken) grease to rub into a sore throat. Toothache we treated by tamping a bit of plug tobacco into a cavity. My father also had a small piece of gum opium that he kept tightly sealed in a glass jar against a really severe toothache; sometimes I toyed with the idea of smoking a little of it. But what I remember best about our kitchen is, of course, all the good things to eat. And one of these I have yet to mention — sourdough pancakes.

All through the winter a butter crock of sourdough batter worked silently on the top step of our cellar stairs. When it was "ripe," my mother began making the pancakes that were our regular winter breakfast fare, and one of the pleasantest memories of my boyhood.

To make them, she took a little of the sourdough batter and broke an egg or two into it. Then she added flour and milk, and perhaps a lump of butter or some bacon drippings. The critical part of the operation was next: the addition of soda. If you added too much, the pancakes would turn yellow and taste of soda; if too little, they would be flat and soggy. With just the right amount, the batter would rise to an almost meringuelike lightness, and the pancakes were all a man or boy could ask of a winter morning. We ate them hot off a soapstone griddle with butter and homemade syrup. Sometimes it took a dozen to stoke a boy up for the start of another day.

CHAPTER SEVEN

Deep Winter

AS WINTER TIGHTENED its iron grip on our town, the ice on the St. Louis, free now of sawlogs, became a broad, glistening highway to the distant logging camps. Every day the tote sleighs (usually called tote teams) would leave Cloquet with their loads of food, wanigan, hay, oats, blacksmith's iron, and other provisions. More than twenty teams were constantly on the river with supplies for the forty-odd logging operations in the deep woods. The music of their big bells came across the ice, round and clear in the thin winter air.

Nobody was ever allowed to ride on a tote sleigh except the driver of the big company horses. But a small boy might imagine himself on the high spring seat beside the teamster, bound for that remote and mysterious world in the endless pine forests. Until he had done a lot of growing, however, he would have to content himself with whatever adventure and diversions he could find at home, and there was, in fact, no end to the ways a boy might pass a pleasant winter day in our town.

At first, as the lakes and ponds began to freeze, we amused ourselves by running on the "rubber ice." When a pond first froze over, the ice would be thin and flexible, so that it would sink a little under your weight, but would not break through unless you remained too long in one spot. The idea was to run across the undulating surface of such a pond fast enough to reach the other side without going through the ice. There were times when you did not quite make it, and this, of course, was what made running on rubber ice interesting.

Later, when the lakes and river froze solidly to a depth of

several feet, we took to skates. Children skated mostly on the lake in Pinehurst Park, holding out their coats like sails to be blown before the wind, and lighting fires on the shore at which to warm themselves. Grown-ups formed gay skating parties and on a Sunday afternoon would skate up the St. Louis as far as the boomhouse, where Joe Dugay would give them coffee and doughnuts.

Our skates were something you would find today, I suppose, only in a museum of Americana. They had rocker blades and four clamps that tightened onto the soles of your shoes by means of a lever in the middle of the skate. There were also two straps that buckled across each foot. In spite of this ingenious arrangement, however, your skates were forever coming loose, always with ignominious results, for there are few things more embarrassing than to be flung flat on the ice in the midst of a fancy figure.

Many older boys, and some of my own age whose folks were richer or more indulgent than mine, had hockey skates. These had thin, straight-edged blades, and you clamped them to your shoes by means of a key you could carry in your pocket. As for skates with blades permanently attached to shoes — the only kind even a tot would recognize today — they were not even imaginable.

One man in our town, a very tall, rawboned Swede called Squeaky Johnson, made a most impressive appearance on a pair of wooden skates with long steel blades that curved up in front. Squeaky was a very good skater, and when he took to the ice, everybody else stopped and watched him perform figure eights and other graceful turns on his quaint Old Country skates.

As soon as there was enough snow on the hills, we made "bumpers" and enjoyed a sport that, so far as I know, was indigenous to our part of the country. To make a bumper you took two apple-barrel staves, cleated them together at each end, and tied a short length of rope to the front cleat. You also needed a couple of feet of broomstick, sharpened at one end. And a hill well covered with snow. At the top of the hill you stood sidewise on your bumper, your feet braced against the cleats, your left hand grasping the rope attached

to the front end. In your right hand you held the pointed
broomstick, which served both to help keep your balance and
steer your course. You gave yourself a push with your right
foot and started down the hill. If it was steep, you were
lucky to reach the bottom still standing up. Bumpering was a
sort of cross between surf-riding and skiing. It took a good
deal of skill and practice to avoid being pitched into a snow-
drift.

In a town with so many Scandinavians and Finns, skiing was
not only a sport but a natural way of getting around in winter.
We skied everywhere, up and down the snow-paved roads,
across the open fields around town, into the woods and
swamps in search of Christmas trees or rabbits. We even skied
to school and left our skiis against the schoolhouse wall in
much the same way bicycles are parked at a suburban school
today.

Our skiis were mostly homemade with the points turned up
over a steampipe at the sawmill. But I always longed for a pair
of Finnish skiis. They were lovely — long and narrow, with a
high crown of polished wood on which was often burned an
intricate design. They were very much like the cross-country
skiis in vogue today, but far more beautiful.

Winter in our town was marked by the complete disappear-
ance of the wheel. After the first freeze-up and snowfall everything moved on runners, including Swan Swanson's cut-
ter, which was drawn by a team of moose.[1] All winter long our
town rang with the music of sleigh bells — the big ones of the
tote teams on the river, the many-toned ones of delivery
sleighs, the cheerful ones of family rigs, even the tinkly bells
on the little cutters in which bundled-up babies were pushed
along the frozen walks. And in a country of steep hills and
great snows, sledding was a sport that everyone from tot to
grown-up could enjoy, each in his own special way.

Our parents and some of the older boys and girls coasted
under the winter stars on Chestnut Hill. Their bobsleds were
long enough to seat a dozen people, each sitting between the
legs of the one behind him and hanging on for dear life to the
ropes that ran alongside the padded seat. It was a long run
down Chestnut Hill, and a bobsled loaded with a dozen per-

sons attained a terrifying speed before it reached the bottom and shot across the railroad tracks at the end of the run. This was not a sport for the fainthearted — nor for children.[2]

Most of us contented ourselves with small sleds, the kind you rode down a hill on your belly and steered by dragging your toes in the snow, right foot if you wanted to go right, and vice versa. My father, who had an ironclad rule never to buy anything you could make for yourself, produced such a sled for me. It was so well made, however, so heavy with iron runners and braces that I was never able to lift it and get a running start at the top of a hill before flopping on my belly for the ride down. So I envied boys with Flexible Flyers, very light sleds that were steered by warping the runners with a sort of wooden handle bar. A boy on a Flexible Flyer could go faster and farther down a hill than one who steered by dragging his toes. But one thing was certain, my homemade sled would outlast them all.

🌲

Between Johnson's pasture and McNeely's hill (the outer boundary of our world) lay Tamarack Swamp. It was a deep muskeg of black spruce and tamarack, so quiet and still that sometimes you had an eerie feeling you were being watched from the shadows. It took a little daring to penetrate very far into Tamarack Swamp. In winter the snow beneath the drooping evergreens was undisturbed except for rabbit tracks. Tamarack Swamp swarmed with rabbits, the kind that are brown in summer but turn white with the approach of winter, called varying hares. You seldom saw them during the day, but on a snapping winter night the swamp must have been alive with them, for their runs were everywhere. These little pathways in the snow, about a handbreadth wide and perhaps a foot deep, led from every direction into wider thoroughfares, which converged into a hard-packed space in the muskeg littered with the tan, pelletlike droppings of the little animals. We used to imagine them holding meetings in these places, or maybe just playing around under the moon.

One of our winter sports was snaring rabbits in Tamarack Swamp. You took a piece of picture wire about three feet long and made a running loop, or noose, at one end. Then you hung the loop in a rabbit run and secured it to an overhanging branch. If you hung the loop just right — not too low or he would jump over it, not too high or he would run under it — a rabbit would be caught in it as he scooted along the run and, more likely than not, you would find him frozen stiff when you picked up your snares the next day.

But not always. Sometimes your snare would be empty, and sometimes you would find a rabbit in it still alive. Then, trying not to look, you would have to hit him with a stick until he was quiet. I cannot say that I cared much for this part of rabbit snaring. And I found it hard to swallow the savory stew my mother would make with the rabbits I brought home from Tamarack Swamp.

We also went to Tamarack Swamp for Christmas trees. In our town, as everywhere else in those days, Christmas was celebrated in a quiet, almost sedate way. The early 1900s were not lacking in business enterprise, but the observance of Christ's birth, at least, had not yet turned into a commercial promotion. Christmas, as I happily remember it, was a time of profound peace and quiet in a small town silenced by a heavy blanket of snow. On Christmas Eve you could hear sleigh bells at an extraordinary distance. To children wide awake in bed there was always the wild surmise that maybe they were Santa's.

For a small boy, however, Christmas did have a certain commercial aspect: it presented him with the problem of how to earn enough money to buy presents for everyone. Billy Horan and I usually went into the Christmas tree business. On Saturdays and after school we trudged through the drifts to Tamarack Swamp with an ax and length of rope. To find a good tree, we usually had to force our way for some distance into the muskeg. After finally selecting and felling one, we attached the rope to it and dragged it back to town. Often it would be dark when we arrived starved and half-frozen. The next day we would canvass the neighborhood, hoping that a customer of previous years would again buy a tree from us. If we were lucky and made a sale, we usually received twenty cents to divide between us.

Even in those days you couldn't buy much for many people at that rate. One year I made only enough from the sale of our trees to buy my mother a pair of scissors for her sewing basket.[3] I had seen them weeks before in the window of Mr. Freeman's jewelry store, and had persuaded him to put them aside for me. They were very interesting scissors in the form of a gilded stork, with the stork's beak functioning as blades.[4]

Each family in Cloquet had its own way of celebrating Christmas, and its own idea of how to decorate a Christmas tree. Ours was set up in the parlor, always in exactly the same spot near the piano, with the same battered Santa Claus at the very top. It was hung with a few German-looking ornaments, carefully preserved in cotton from Christmas to Christmas, and with garlands of popcorn and cranberries we had gathered in a swamp across the river. Besides paper chains, the decorations also included pink popcorn balls, oranges, and apples. It was at Christmas that the oranges made their sole appearance in our house. The apples on the tree looked oddly special and unfamiliar, although they were really no different from those we ate every winter evening.

Our tree was lighted with little candles of different colors clipped to the branches in tin basins to catch the drippings. They gave a soft, wavering light to the dim parlor on Christmas morning, and a smell of balsam boughs warmed by their tiny flames. On Christmas Eve candles were also placed in the parlor windows of houses all over Cloquet — to light the way of the Christ child, it was said. The effect of so many candles gleaming between the lace curtains of dark windows was very pretty on a snowy night.

Christmases in our town may not have been so different from those in other homes and other towns around the turn of the century. But in a few minor ways they may have been unique. I could not think of our own holiday season without recalling us children trooping to the Company Store on Christmas morning to receive a shiny little dinner pail — just like our fathers' — filled with candies as a gift from the lumber company; the highly polished apple left under the tree for Santa and how we marveled, when we were younger, at the big bite taken out of it; the excitement of going to the Railway Express office with my sled to haul home the box of presents from our aunts in the Twin Cities; the freezing walk to church with my mother for midnight Mass on Christmas Eve; and the feeling of incompleteness and sadness with my father "up in the woods" and his place at the table empty for Christmas dinner.

During the long northern winters, there were times when it was just too cold even to build snow forts, skate on Skinn Lake, or snare rabbits. Then, with no television to watch, what did a boy do to pass the time after school or of a winter evening? To tell the truth, I find it a bit hard to remember.

With their dolls and toy kitchens and all, girls did not seem to have much trouble filling the indoor hours, but after chores and homework a small boy might find it difficult to occupy himself until bedtime. We had games (mostly hold-over Christmas presents) like tiddlywinks, jackstraws, and fishpond. Cards — Old Maid and a game we imagined to be poker. Checkers, of course, but you became pretty bored with these diversions toward the end of winter, so Billy Horan and I turned to chess.

From reading books on chivalry, Billy and I developed a powerful longing to play chess like the knights of old. My Aunt Vic gave me a chess set for Christmas, and since there was nobody in Cloquet to teach us, we learned to play the game from the eleventh edition of the *Encyclopaedia Britannica* in the public library. Our game had one special feature, how-ever, not to be found in the official rules. In emulation of the knightly players, the loser always made at least a token at-tempt to break the chessboard over the winner's head.

When nothing better offered, we would occasionally turn to the stereoscope. Although the scenes were all as familiar as the roses on our parlor rug, there never ceased to be some-thing magical in the transformation of ordinary pictures into three-dimensional ones so lifelike that "you could almost walk into them." Of all the pictures in our collection — the life of Christ, foreign views, comic scenes, and so on — I seem, for some reason I cannot explain, to remember best some Easter lilies against a maroon background with the legend, "Consider the Lilies of the Field." I guess I thought them beautiful.

Even more fascinating were the magic lantern shows. We ourselves did not own a magic lantern, but sometimes we would be invited to see some new slides from Sears, Roebuck at a neighbor's house. We sat in the neighbor's parlor in silent anticipation, our sense of wonder heightened by the unfamiliarity of the hushed and darkened room. Finally, a ray of light from the smoking lantern pierced the darkness, and there on a bed sheet pinned to the wall was a picture of the Russo-Japanese War! Marvel followed marvel, battle scenes and warships were succeeded by tranquil views of European scenery and classical ruins, and finally by some hilarious slides of "Fun at the Beach." Nothing, not even the crack across Admiral Dewey's mustache or a "View of the Bay of Naples" upside down, could dispel the wonder of it all.

In addition to such home diversions, we occasionally enjoyed shows and entertainments during the winter in Nelson's Opera House.[5] B. J. Summerfield's clothing store occupied the first floor of the opera house, but the second was available for political rallies, graduation exercises, and other civic and cultural events, including home talent shows that on one memorable occasion ended in a riot. It was on the stage of Nelson's Opera House that I joined, with a distinct feeling of nausea, in singing our eighth-grade graduation song:

> On, gallop along, my true and trusty steed,
>   On, gallop along, nor fail me in my need.
> At love and duty's call, I'll ride what e're
>   befall,
>   On, on, my gallant steed, my gallant
>   steed speed on.

Nelson's Opera House also accommodated any stray band of entertainers that happened to make a one-night stand in Cloquet. Among these were hypnotists, a class of showmen once quite popular in small towns like ours. One of them

displayed a blond female in deep sleep in the window of
Proulx's drugstore.[6] Even at our early age we sensed something obscene about this, and stole only furtive glances at the
corpselike form in the window.

On rare occasions a vaudeville show came to Cloquet with
song and dance teams, slapstick comedians, and (also popular) female impersonators. I saw no more than two or three of
these shows, and I can recall distinctly only one piece of business from any of them: a soft-shoe dance man who recited
between his turns the following imperishable lines:

> Now Shakespeare says that nothing's right
> or wrong.
> I think he's right, I think he's right.
> And yet, if nothing's right or wrong,
> Why Shakespeare may be wrong.
> I think he's right, I think he's right.

Minstrel shows sometimes came to town, and once a traveling company presented Gilbert and Sullivan's *H.M.S. Pin-
afore*. I can also remember a musical comedy troupe complete
with chorus girls, but I am unable to report on its merits since
it was rated X by my parents. I recall, however, that a boy in
high school became wildly infatuated with one of the show
girls, and that his people had a hard time restraining him
from following the show out of town.

In addition to live entertainment, primitive one-reel movies
began to be shown at the opera house. It was there that I saw
The Great Train Robbery, although the film resembled nothing
so much as a heavy Minnesota blizzard, and I am not sure that
I actually *saw* the robbery at all. Later on movies were shown
at the Bijou, a theater owned by Frank Gumm (Judy
Garland's father) which was located over Kuitu & Mattinen's
store. When films for the current show failed to arrive from
Duluth on "Gilbert's train," a boy went through town with a
megaphone announcing, "No show tonight! No show
tonight!"[7]

Several times during the winter, the more sophisticated and
well-heeled citizens of Cloquet hired a special train to take
them to the opera or theater in Duluth and return with them
on the same night. On a really memorable occasion I myself

journeyed to Duluth to see Sarah Bernhardt in scenes from *The Merchant of Venice*. It is perhaps significant that, while I remember absolutely nothing about how I got to Duluth or with whom I went, I do recall vividly the Divine Sarah reclining on a couch in a crimson robe and making Portia's immortal plea for mercy in a voice that nobody, not even a small boy become an old man, could ever forget.[8]

🌲

Winter was the time when boys in Cloquet, for want of anything better to do, got in most of their reading, although a lot of them had no more interest in the printed word than do today's young television watchers. We all managed, however, to keep up with the comic-strip doings of the Katzenjammer Kids, Mutt and Jeff, Jiggs and Maggie, and Happy Hooligan (who was beginning to look a little old-fashioned), passing around the "funny papers" until they were worn out. Most of us had a few dime novels stashed away in a secret place. For some obscure reason, parents considered such sterling characters as the Merriwell brothers a bad influence on growing boys, and literature dealing with their exploits was almost universally proscribed. There existed, however, a widespread dime novel underground and by careful concealment and clandestine swapping a boy managed to do quite a lot of illicit reading.

For something on a higher level we visited the public library on Cloquet Avenue. We perused eagerly and knew the exact days on which *Life* and *Judge* (both humorous *Punch*-type magazines at that time) appeared in the reading room. We also flipped through the pages of the *Youth's Companion* and *St. Nicholas* and were occasionally stopped by a story — if the pictures were exciting. I myself did a good deal of reading in such adult magazines as *Scribner's, Century,* and *Everybody's* — most of them now long since dead. But of all that I must have read with the avid interest of youth, I must report in some bewilderment that I remember only one fragment of a single magazine article: a piece on physical fitness, in which the author noted that waiters carried trays

with chin up and eyes straight ahead, and that this was somehow good for one's posture.

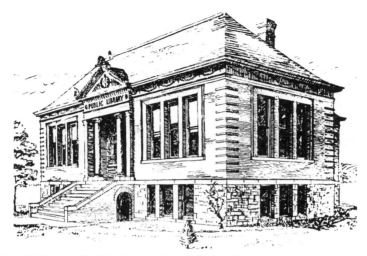

*The old Cloquet Public Library in which I whiled away many a pleas-
ant hour in undirected reading.*

Then came the day when I discovered the open stacks, and
suddenly there it all was, ready and waiting! With nobody to
guide me, I took off in all directions and no doubt wasted a
great deal of valuable young time. Surely there must have
been something wrong in devouring the works of Thomas H.
Huxley and H. Rider Haggard with equal enthusiasm. Yet I
doubt that a directed course of reading would have given me
nearly as much pleasure or the joy, for example, that comes
from an accidental meeting with a Huckleberry Finn or even
a Peck's Bad Boy.

   If I were asked to name my favorite author of that time, I
am afraid I should have to mention the forgotten creator of
the *Deerfoot Series,*[9] a continuing saga of a "good Indian" who
carried a Bible that at least once in each volume stopped an
enemy bullet. I enjoyed with the utmost indiscrimination Jack
London, Mark Twain, Richard Harding Davis, Jules Verne,

Horatio Alger, and Lew Wallace. I recall that I found James Fenimore Cooper, G. A. Henty, and Sir Walter Scott boring, and that I thought too many things happened fortuitously in the *Swiss Family Robinson*. But it had to be a dull book, indeed, that could not carry me from cover to cover.

All in all, it could not be said that winter in our town was a bad time for a small boy. When you are ten, you don't seem to mind the cold too much. You are like the Indian in Canada my father used to tell about. A white man asked him, "Aren't you cold, with all that bare skin?" "Is your face cold?" the Indian asked. "No," the white man admitted. "Well, I'm all face," the Indian said.

So we played, hunted, trapped, explored, built snow forts, fought snowball battles, skated, skied, and coasted, all without paying much attention to a cold that would have anchored us in later years close to the kitchen range. It was only at night, I seem to remember, that we felt the chill, cowering in our flannel nightshirts under icy blankets.

There were extra chores for boys to perform in winter. But shoveling snow, carrying coal and wood in and ashes out, sprouting potatoes, and keeping the lamps filled and polished were no more onerous than mowing the lawn in summer, or stacking firewood, or picking potato bugs on a hot afternoon. About the only thing wrong with our winters, in fact, was their excessive length. After six months or so of short, dark days and unremitting cold, even a small boy grew a little weary of the sight of snow. And, as winter drew toward a close, its rigors became more and more irksome.

For one thing, the quality of our food supply deteriorated markedly. The vegetables in our cellar sprouted and wilted, our hens stopped laying eggs, and as we scraped the bottom of our meat chest, the Irish stew began to contain more and more potatoes and less and less pork. Sometimes our barrels of apples gave out altogether.

Winter, too, was the season of sickness, of coughs, colds, sniffles, and also more serious illnesses. It was the time when my sister Frances had diphtheria and almost died of it, and when my mother lay delirious with fever, and I prayed for her in the woodshed. With my father away in the woods and often completely out of touch, I think we felt a little helpless in the face of life's perils. Even my mother's stout heart, I suspect, sometimes failed her a little.

So although we had hailed the first snowfall with such joy, the time came when we waited for the end of winter with an impatience that sometimes approached despair. And "Doc's" joke about summer beginning at 11:35 and winter setting in at 5:47 did not seem very funny any more.

CHAPTER EIGHT

Spring At Last!

SPRING was a brief season along the St. Louis River, and not all of its aspects were charming. The *Pine Knot* complained about the heaps of garbage uncovered by the melting drifts and about cows roaming loose through the streets.[1] The whole town had a rather seedy look after its long hibernation. Still, the fresh green of the willows along Otter Creek was lovely; sparkling rivulets of melted snow water ran down the streets; robins bobbed cheerfully about the yard; and in the pinewoods west of town the trailing arbutus came into bloom.

Gathering arbutus was a custom that amounted almost to a springtime rite in our town. The little flower with its shiny leaves and pink blossoms was to be found in the few stands of pine spared by the logger's ax. It was the first flower of spring, often opening while the snow still lay in the shadows of the forest, and people used to make up little parties and go to the pine groves to gather arbutus. It was a sort of ritual celebration of winter's end.

Another pleasant springtime custom was the children's observance of May Day. On the first day of May they wove little baskets with colored strips of paper, making them as gay as they knew how. They filled these baskets with spring flowers — wild violets, perhaps — or with homemade candy; then they hung them on the front doors of friends or neighbors, rang the bell, and scurried away. I have never heard of this charming custom being practiced anywhere except in our town.

Our real spring festival was Easter. It was not much different from Easter anywhere else, I suppose, except that it was apt to be celebrated with snow on the ground. In kitchens everywhere it was preceded by the bustling activity of dyeing Easter eggs, and there was something quite fascinating about seeing eggs out of your own henhouse in gorgeous shades of pink, green, blue, and yellow. Small children made nests of their clothes on Easter Eve, and in the morning found them filled with these same eggs and perhaps a few chocolate bunnies or a downy little duck. Women wore their new hats to church on Easter no matter what the weather, and if you were lucky enough to get a new suit or pair of shoes during the year, Easter was when you got them.

The only other spring holiday was the one we now call Memorial Day. It was originated to honor the Civil War dead, and people had a vague feeling that something was amiss when young Spanish-American War veterans began to march in the parade. Only four decades had passed since the silence fell at Appomattox, and Decoration Day (as we called it then) was still a day of quiet, almost sad observance. After the morning parade down Arch Street in which we school children marched with little flags, people went to the cemeteries and placed flowers on the graves of Civil War veterans. A squad of Spanish-American War vets fired three rounds from their Springfields, and someone played taps on his bugle. Most people spent the rest of the holiday at a quiet family picnic in Pinehurst Park. Except for school being out and marching in the parade, Decoration Day was not a very special event in the life of a small boy.[2]

It was not by the calendar that the arrival of spring was marked, but by the opening of the marble season. Before winter had really departed, we began to play "plunk." We would find a spot on the south side of a building like Bill Sarette's store, where the sun had laid the ground bare, and scratch a circle about a yard in diameter.[3] Into this circle each player would drop a marble. Then from a lag line about ten feet away, each in turn would try to knock marbles out of the ring with a crockery sphere about the size of a golf ball called a "plunker." Any marbles you plunked out of the ring, you kept.

Plunk was a good enough game while the ground was too cold and wet to "knuckle down," but as soon as the earth warmed up a bit, the regular game of marbles, or "mibs," took over. The fascination of marbles, I think, lay in the fact that, while it was a good game of skill, it also held out the lure of material gain. Marbles were always played for "keeps," and a kid could get rich at the game.[4]

I don't mean that marbles were ever played for money, but a good shooter could become immensely wealthy in that strange currency of commies, aggies, glassies, crockies, chinees, and so on. Like money or poker chips, each marble had a universally recognized value. A chinee was worth a set number of commies (the lowest unit of value), a crockie so many chinees, a glassie a certain number of crockies, etc. I have forgotten the exact table of values, but I do remember that an aggie, which was always a player's shooter, had a high value to be determined only by bargaining and swapping. Some aggies were beautiful specimens of chalcedony, so beautiful that they were never actually played with for fear of chipping them. I remember one of my own as I would re- member a precious stone.

The Romans played marbles as kids, and I have half a dozen round stone pellets from an Egyptian tomb that look suspiciously like the "mibs" I knew as a boy. I would not be surprised if the game played with them in the shadow of the pyramids was governed by pretty much the same rules as those we observed in the lee of Bill Sarette's store.

Despite the championship matches one still reads about in the papers, I have a feeling that the ancient pastime is at last on its way out. I have friends who now collect marbles as items of Americana. As I inspect their jars of antique commies, crockies, chinees, and glassies, I realize sadly that these are the selfsame "mibs" I played with — not so very long ago, it seems to me.

On windy spring days we flew kites. They were not the gaudy, tridimensional, tailless affairs with stressed skin struc- ture and scientific compression tension that kids put into the air nowadays, but simple, homemade kites that differed from one another only in size, never in design.

To make a kite, you crossed two strips of wood whittled thin with your jackknife, and bound them together with the strongest thread in your mother's sewing basket. Then you ran a piece of twine around the notched ends of the sticks and pulled it taut. This provided you with a very light but strong frame onto which you pasted a piece of newspaper with flour-and-water paste. You now had a kite complete except for the tail, which consisted of a long piece of cloth with short pieces tied to it crosswise at about ten-inch intervals. In a day when everything from worn-out sheets to outgrown pants was hoarded to make rag rugs, it was not always easy for a boy to come by enough cloth for a proper kite tail.

With a friend to hold the kite for you, you let out about twenty feet of store twine and ran against the wind. Your friend released the kite, and it was air borne; that is to say, it immediately became a live and often perverse thing. If the tail was too short, it would dart crazily about and finally plunge to the ground. If too long, it would sink ignominiously to earth of its own weight. You had to be a good judge of tails.

In my boyhood, before there were airplanes flying at 30,000 feet without getting a glance, there was something wonderful about soaring vicariously to the tremendous heights a kite attained in a good wind. Perhaps it was the fascination of having actual physical contact with something so distant from the earth, of feeling the tug of the kite in your arms, as if it wanted to lift you off the ground and have you join it in the immense sky.

We also played a game with kites. We sent "messengers" up the kite string. The messenger was a disk of paper with a small hole in the middle. You tore the paper from the outer edge to the hole, slipped it over the string, and let the wind carry it up to the kite. Sometimes we had races to see whose messenger would arrive first. But winning wasn't important. It was enough to see your messenger skitter up the string to that distant, swaying object so far from earth.

Seasonal events, often disastrous, recur in the life of many towns to provide material for the kind of adult reminiscence a boy overhears and senses to be of epic gravity. Among these are floods, tornadoes, earthquakes, and other acts of God. Around our town forest fires threatened every fall, and a tragic one in 1894 killed over two hundred people in the nearby village of Hinckley.[5] This was still much talked about, but the standard topic of old-timers' yarns was the famous log jams.

These occurred almost every spring when the logs from the camps on the St. Louis and its tributaries — the Cloquet, Embarrass, and Whiteface — were floated down to the mills. At best the drive, as it was called, was a difficult, man-killing, and frequently dangerous operation. At worst it wound up in a jam. If the water was fast, a few logs hung up on a rock; then thousands more piled up in a great tangled mass. There was nothing that frantic peavey work or a foreman's curses could do to halt the build up.

The technique of breaking a jam was to find the "key log" in the gigantic jackstraw snarl and loosen it with peaveys or, if necessary, dynamite.[6] When the key log was dislodged, the cry "She hauls!" went up, and the whole towering structure collapsed with an awesome roar. Twenty-foot sawlogs hurtled into the air as the writhing mass surged ahead. Now the riverman at work on the jam was confronted with a fresh problem: how to save his life. Usually he made it ashore before the avalanche could overwhelm him. But sometimes he was forced to "ride it out." This meant that he had to balance himself and keep his footing on a twisting, pitching log as it swept ahead of the jam. A famous ballad entitled "The Jam on Gerry's Rock" celebrated the heroic death of Young Jack Monroe, a foreman who tried to ride it out and failed.[7]

I often heard my father tell of the great jam at Independence on the Cloquet River, and how a river boss named Jack Chisholm declared that he would drive every log in the Cloquet in forty days or eat what was left. The logs, however, got ahead of the water and piled up so high at Independence that it required a month's time and $40,000 in wages and dynamite to break the jam. Jack Chisholm's diet was for a long time afterward the subject of many a sly and sometimes ribald jest.

I remember, too, the drive foreman who boasted that with a case of dynamite and another of John Jameson whisky he would break the 1904 jam at the Narrows[8] or blow himself up in the attempt — and did. Almost every spring provided a new log jam story, and I listened to my elders tell these tales in much the same way, I imagine, that a youngster on the frontier hung on stories of Indian raids or buffalo hunts.

Whatever the law may have been for grown-ups, kids opened the fishing season as soon as the ice was out of Otter Creek. Izaak Walton observed that "Rivers and the Inhabitants of the watery Element were made for wise men to contemplate, and fools to pass by without consideration," and he might just as well have said "boys" instead of "wise men."[9] For every small boy there is a special fascination in trying to catch things that live in the water — denizens, as it were, of a strange and alien world. They need be only frogs, tadpoles, crayfish, or the odd little creatures looking something like sea horses to be found in rain barrels. But nothing, obviously, compares with real fish.

We fished hopefully for speckled trout in Otter Creek with very small hooks — even bent pins — baited with a worm. But we seldom coaxed a nibble from anything larger than silvery, sardine-size fish we called shiners. They skillfully ate our worms without ever touching the hook, and I cannot recall catching one. But Otter Creek was such a lovely stream in spring, meandering through lush meadows and clumps of willow, that it was enough just to feed the shiners — always with the hope, of course, that someday we would catch a speckled beauty.

The St. Louis River, which one might expect to offer better sport, was singularly uninhabited by anything but bullheads, red horse, and a few rock bass. The red horse were not much respected as edible fare in our town, but we fished for them, nevertheless, with as many fat angleworms as could be festooned on a hook. After spitting on the bait for good luck, we dangled it in the water from a long bamboo pole.

Red horse may not have been very good eating, but they were quite a handsome fish with rosy scales, and some were a good size. I shall never forget the pride with which I toted home my first red horse, with its tail switching along the ground. It was, after all, the first fish I ever caught.

When spring finally came to our town, my mother was sure to say one day, "It looks like we're going to have some nice warm weather for awhile. I think we should have Jenny Smith to dinner." So when I think of spring in Cloquet, I think of Jenny Smith. Not because she was an important person, but because she was the kind a boy would find interesting and remember.

There *were* persons in Cloquet, of course, whose importance would impress even a small boy. Like Sherman Coy, an executive of the lumber company who had been a famous Yale end, and an even greater player, some said, than his better-known brother Ted Coy. And I remember R. M. Weyerhaeuser. He was what my father called a "commoner." He addressed my father by his first name, and I recall him listening seriously, on one occasion, while my father gave him some practical advice on how to run his already vast enterprise.[10]

But the people I can recall most clearly were those like the teamster in the lumberyard who sometimes allowed us to drive his nags from atop a load of pine planks; a bookkeeper in the Company office, who spent every evening of his life trying to invent a perpetual motion machine; a dentist who played shortstop on our baseball team and always bunted because, while he wasn't much good at bat, he could run very fast.

Like every other small town, Cloquet had its cast of stock characters. There was the "horrible example," who had once studied for the priesthood (it was said). The town fat man who despite his three hundred-odd pounds, most of it around the waist, had sired a fine brood of children. The town idiot was called Parasol Jack, because he was never seen, rain or shine, summer or winter, without a large umbrella. And there was Pants Mary, a recluse on the outskirts of town who appeared on the streets only rarely, and always in a logger's stagged pants.

I remember Gracie Parker especially, because of her long hair and all the trouble it caused her. My father belonged to the Woodmen of the World, a fraternal order that provided life insurance for its members, and he would send me to pay his premiums to Gracie's father, who was treasurer of the Cloquet lodge. I can recall how small she looked as she wrote out the receipt by lamplight, with her dark hair falling almost to her feet, like the sisters in the Danderine ads.[11] She was so tiny, people said, because all her growth was "going to her hair." So Gracie let them cut it off at last, and then stayed in the house for a long time, ashamed to go out and be stared at; because in those times a short-haired woman was considered peculiar, to say the least. People waited to see if Gracie would grow any taller after sacrificing her hair, but she never did.

I am afraid I have been digressing; let us get back to Jenny Smith. Jenny was sort of the town invalid. Nobody knew why she was bedridden, but a long time ago she had been taken sick, went to bed with whatever ailed her, and just never got up again.[12]

Jenny's bedroom faced Third Street, and you could see her and wave to her as you passed her house on your way downtown. She was a rather pretty young woman, with smooth dark hair and brown eyes that looked very large in her pale face. Her paleness, of course, was from having lain in bed for so long and never getting any fresh air or sun, except when she went visiting in her wheel chair.

People naturally felt sorry for Jenny, and there was a sort of community effort to lighten the boredom of her confinement. Neighbors brought her jellies or perhaps half a newly baked angel cake, and when spring came they began having her to dinner.

Women put themselves out when they had Jenny to dinner, probably so that she would tell other women what a wonderful table Mrs. So-and-so set — which Jenny never failed to do. Once I went with my father to fetch her to our house. He and

Jenny's father lifted her out of bed and into a wheel chair, then we pushed her up Third Street with people greeting her along the way and Jenny responding gaily. She was a cheerful girl that everyone liked and wanted to "do for." So many people brought her delicacies and invited her out, in fact, that she became quite a well-rounded invalid — "plump as a pa'tridge," my father said. Some people said that Jenny didn't have it all that bad.

Different doctors examined Jenny and, although various theories were advanced, none could say why she was unable to walk. Finally a young doctor from St. Paul, who happened to be visiting in Cloquet, was persuaded to take a look at her. After a thorough examination, he expressed the opinion that nothing at all was the matter with Jenny. She had been really sick at one time, it appeared, and after a prolonged spell in bed, she just hadn't felt like getting up. Finally she couldn't, even if she had wanted to. The young doctor, who must have been a bit of a psychologist, took an interest in her case and put her on a regimen that got Jenny up at last, as chipper as anybody.[13]

Or perhaps there was more to it than that. At the risk of sounding like a shameless inventor of happy endings, I must add that in the course of all this, the young doctor from St. Paul fell in love with Jenny and married her.

🌲

For our family, my mother and sisters and me, the great event of spring was, of course, the return of my father from the woods. As the camps began to break and their crews to trickle into town, we waited impatiently for him to appear. Except for a few letters brought down by the tote team, we had been out of touch with him since before Christmas. To a child, a parent can grow to be almost a stranger in so long a time.

When my father did come back, it was usually unannounced. Maybe it was while my mother was cooking dinner and I was carrying in wood for the woodbox in the kitchen. He would appear suddenly, perhaps at the back door, with his packsack on his back and a growth of beard on his weather-reddened face that made him look unfamiliar, strange. My father was the most undemonstrative of men, but at this one time of the year, he reacted almost gaily to the joyful storm of welcome that broke around him. Then, after the excitement had died down, he might fish from the bottom of his turkey a small muslin bag and hand it to us carelessly. It contained spruce gum he had gathered from the trees at camp, nuggets of grayish-pink resin that turned to pink chewing gum in your mouth. It tasted like resin, and that is to say not very good, but we chewed it and pretended to enjoy it. After all, there wasn't much he could bring us from the woods as a home-coming present.

So my father was at home with us for a little while, but it was not long before the sawmills got up steam, the whine of the band saws could be heard along the river, and smoke from the tall burners drifted over Cloquet again. Spring came to its abrupt end. The mill crews went back to work, school let out, and a boy's long summer began.

CHAPTER NINE

To Kill A Summer's Day

THE FIRST DAY of summer, I suppose, was the day we "went barefoot." There was no set date for the change-over from shoes to bare feet, like straw-hat day with adults. It occurred simultaneously among all boys and many girls, as if by some instinct such as told the birds when to start north in spring.

You ventured out rather gingerly at first, with feet made tender by a long winter in shoe leather, but with a joyous response to direct contact with mother earth. I seem to remember that we leaped and shouted in a sort of ecstasy of release. And now only one other ritual of the summer solstice remained: to go to the barbershop and get shingled by Mr. Moody, who took a pair of clippers and cropped your hair to the scalp. After that winter was really and truly behind you, and with its exit came a freedom of spirit that only a small boy could ever know.

Not that he didn't still have certain responsibilities. There were chores to perform even in summer — like, for instance, keeping the kitchen range in fuel. Ours used firewood from the mills. It was delivered in big box wagons drawn by two heavy draft horses. The wagon box — as large as one of our bedrooms, it seemed — tipped up and dumped a huge heap of firewood in the street before our house. It was my job to move it, wheelbarrow by wheelbarrow, to the back yard and stack it in neat piles to dry. One summer, I recall with painful precision, I wheeled and stacked fourteen loads. And I can still feel the sinking of my heart when, coming home from somewhere on a fine summer day — a day just right for squirrel hunting on McNeely's hill — I would find a new mountain of firewood waiting for me.

There were not many ways a boy could earn money during the summer in Cloquet. Farmers sometimes paid as much as fifty cents a day for picking rocks off their fields or weeding their truck gardens. Makers of bluing (an indigo preparation women put in their washes to make them white) engaged boys to sell their product from door to door. If you picked more berries than your mother needed for canning, you could generally sell the surplus to neighbors. And a few fortunate boys had paper routes.

You could also sell magazine subscriptions. Instead of stuffing mailboxes with elaborate promotional literature, publishers hired small boys to pester people to subscribe. One of them ran an ad in a magazine with the headline: "THE PRETTIEST GIRL IN IOWA WANTS YOU TO WORK FOR HER." In return for selling a dozen subscriptions to her magazine, the ad promised a genuine Hamilton single-shot .22-caliber rifle with blued-steel barrel and hand-rubbed oiled walnut stock. This combination of feminine lure and my yearning for a gun that would shoot real bullets proved irresistible. I finally sold the twelve subscriptions, sent the money to "the prettiest girl in Iowa" (thinking how pleased she would be with me), and received the Hamilton rifle.

But for the most part, work was hard to find in our town, summer days were long, and a boy's chief problem was apt to be how to kill the dragging hours. Aside from baseball, swimming, hunting, and the like, we contrived to do it in various and ingenious ways — ways, I am sure, with which small boys are still familiar.

We made slip-whistles from green willow twigs, red ink from a little forest flower whose name I do not know, wintergreen tea (and drank it cold), little pipes from acorns and a bit of straw. We played mumblety-peg, one old cat, and duck-on-the rock.[1] We walked fences, whittled wooden chains (seldom successfully), caught frogs and tadpoles, flushed out gophers, imprisoned fireflies under a jelly glass, searched for four-leaf clovers. Even less productively we spent idle hours watching water bugs skate on the glassy surface of a still pond or a hawk wheeling in the pale summer sky. We made grass-hoppers "spit tobacco," and sent ladybugs flying home to rescue their children from a burning house.

Sometimes we experimented with the grown-up business of smoking, a rather reckless venture at a time when cigarettes were called "coffin nails." Not until we were older did we actually try smoking tobacco. As small boys we puffed away at cigarettes rolled (in a piece of newspaper) from corn silk, coffee, tea, and the dried leaves of a weed we fondly sup-posed to be wild tobacco. More daringly we sometimes ex-perimented with a kind of cigarette that older people, mostly women, smoked for asthma: I believe they were called Cubebs. And in lieu of snuff we tucked into our cheek some-thing called coffee essence, probably the "instant" coffee of that day. Fortunately, none of this was either habit-forming or even something you would want to try more than once.

Sometimes we went adventuring. As opposed to marbles, say, or baseball, adventuring did not demand any competitive effort; it did not even require having anything in mind. You simply started out with a friend or two for the woods, or the reservation, or maybe just the cow pasture at the end of the street. You didn't expect anything special to happen, and often nothing did. But usually you could catch a few frogs, flush a gopher out of his hole, or maybe find a nest of baby field mice. And occasionally you stumbled on to something really odd or mysterious.

There was the time we came across the poster Joe Lajoie had put up against his enemy Pete Cadotte.[2] Joe and Pete were excitable French Canadians (the kind some people called "Jumping Frenchmen") who had feuded in our town for years. Any chance meeting on the street was sure to lead to threats of violence and torrents of insult in patois French. Joe's poster, however, was in English. It was printed on pink paper in big black type like an auction poster, and it was tacked to a stump in the Company's horse pasture. It read:

P. CADOTTE IS A SKUNK AND A SCOUNDREL

*He is a liar and a spreader
of dirty lies, and he should
have his tongue cut out*

There was a lot more I cannot remember, and at the end of it all Joe signed his name and dared Pete to meet him man to man. It was something a grown-up might have laughed at, I suppose. But to a small boy there was nothing funny in this ugly outpouring of adult hatred; the fine summer day seemed suddenly less sunny and beautiful.

Another time Billy Horan and I were adventuring along the river, looking for crayfish on the shore opposite the Island. We did not consider these crayfish good to eat, but if you smashed one between two stones and found some little white, buttonlike disks, you put them in your pocket and carried them as good-luck charms. While we were busy looking for crayfish in the blue river mud, we saw a big man in a white apron come out of one of the saloons on the Island. He was carrying a smaller man in his arms. He carried him, feebly kicking, to the river embankment and held him over a railing above the water. He was saying something to the man, but we could not hear what. After a while the big man turned and dropped the little one onto the ground and went back into the saloon.

All the way home we speculated on the meaning of this strange episode. We had been frightened for the man struggling in the big man's arms over the water. But it was a special kind of fright, one mixed with wonder and puzzlement and a disturbing mistrust of what went on in that mysterious grown-up world beyond our years.

Sometimes on a summer day we would hang around Joe Phelion's blacksmith shop, hoping for a chance to steal a horseshoe nail.[3] When I think of Joe's smithy, I remember most vividly its smells: the smell of the charcoal fire in his forge, of burning iron, of red-hot horseshoes being pressed against horses' hooves (like feathers burning), and — when you got near enough to him — the smell of Joe himself. Joe would let us pump the great leather bellows while he turned a shoe in the glowing coals on his forge, but we seldom had any conversation with him.

I don't suppose you could say we really stole any horseshoe nails from the small wooden kegs that stood around Joe's smithy. Joe knew when we filched one, but he never let on. So it wasn't really stealing, although we liked to think it was.

Once you had it in your pocket, there were several interesting things you could do with a horseshoe nail. You could stick it through a cork, add three chicken tail feathers, and have a dart to throw at a wall. You could hammer it around a steel rod and make a finger ring that was reputed to give strength to your arm or, if you were old, to ward off rheumatism. Or you could take a couple of nails to the railroad track and make a pair of scissors.

You climbed the high bank of the right of way (it was covered with morning glories early in the day) and placed two crossed nails on the shiny rail. Then you waited for an ore train to come along from the iron range. In theory, the nails would be flattened and welded together beneath the wheels into a miniature pair of scissors. But it never worked out that way. If you found the nails at all after the train had passed, they would be merely misshapen bits of metal. This, however, did not destroy our belief that a pair of scissors could result. We kept on trying, just as we kept on putting horsehairs in the rain barrel in the belief that they would turn into snakes, looking for a little horse at the center of every jawbreaker (it always turned out to be a caraway seed), or expecting stump water to eradicate warts. Repeated experimental disproof seemed to have no effect on such boyhood faiths; sometimes I half believe in them to this day.

Although our parents darkly forbade us to do it, we also dropped in occasionally to visit with Louie Hurtig, and hear him tell how he had worked a dynamite gun at San Juan Hill

An early view of the dalles of the St. Louis River taken in the 1880s soon after logging began.

The falls of the "big, wide, root beer" St. Louis River as they looked in the 1890s.

In the winter most of the men left Cloquet for the logging camps. This is the crew of Brevator Camp 6 during the winter of 1907–08.

Life in the logging camps was crude, lonely, and sometimes dangerous for the men of Cloquet. This is the cook shanty at the J. M. Paine Company camp in 1899.

A load of logs from the "Roaring Stoney" camp on a snowy road near Cloquet, about 1910.

Logs from forty-odd camps in the pinewoods kept Cloquet's sawmills going all summer. In the background is the Northern Lumber Company's mill about 1910.

Endless stacks of lumber formed a sort of wooden city with plank-paved streets and grassy alleys between the tall, leaning piles. In the background is the Cloquet Lumber Company's mill about 1910.

Trucks of lumber ready for the planers jammed the track-lined yard of the Johnson-Wentworth Company's mill in Cloquet about 1910.

The fire department on Avenue C is shown with its new horse-drawn equipment used to fight fires in the wooden town of Cloquet about 1905. At the left is Grunig's Meat Market. The fireman (inset) is not identified.

At the turn of the century Cloquet was a small, rough sawmill town in northern Minnesota. "Company houses" still predominated in the older section.

On Memorial Day in the eary 1900s everyone in town followed the parade to the cemetery and decorated the graves of Civil War veterans. Note the office of the Pine Knot (left) and the many woodpiles (right) at the intersection of Broadway and Avenue C.

A Fourth of July crowd gathered for the log-rolling contests in Pinehurst Park in the early 1900s. The traditional bateau on the lake held the officials and birlers.

Judge F. A. Watkins (right) of Carlton County, in which Cloquet is located, went for a spin with his family in a 1907 "International."

A Sunday outing at Chub Lake, the popular picnic spot about six miles from Cloquet, was a high light of the summer. As this photograph taken about 1905 shows, swimming was the biggest attraction for the youngsters.

In 1918 a great forest fire destroyed Cloquet. Only one public building, the Garfield School, and a few houses withstood the holocaust. Photo by Olson Studio, Cloquet, taken soon after the fire.

The Northwestern Paper Mill in Cloquet after the 1918 fire.

in the Spanish-American War. He was a grimy character, with a drooping mustache and a shiny steel hook at the end of his right arm. He told us his hand had been shot off in the war, but everyone knew he had lost it in a mill accident.

We liked to hear Louie tell about his adventures, even though we knew most of them were made up. Once we watched hungrily while he cooked a huge beefsteak on the top of his stove, flipping it over with his hook. On summer evenings the volunteer fire department would sometimes practice on Louie's shack. This was before the town had a horse-drawn fire engine. The volunteers would come charging down the street pulling their pumper by long ropes. While six men manned the pump handles, others would throw up ladders, climb onto the roof, and pretend to be putting out a fire. This struck us as amusing, and we would cheer derisively when a little water spurted from the hose. Finally Louie's shack actually did catch on fire and the *Pine Knot* reported that the fire company "responded with celerity" — but not in time to save the shack from burning to the ground.[4]

In 1909 the *Pine Knot* further reported that Louie had gone to Duluth, where, "after a prolonged spree" he shot himself through the head in a hotel room.

$$\uparrow$$

But I would not want to leave the impression that we spent all the days of summer skylarking around the countryside with nothing constructive in mind, or visiting with interesting town characters. In late summer we spent a good many industrious days picking the wild berries my mother put up as "sauces" for our winter desserts.

Of an early August morning, perhaps with some neighbors' children, we would start for the berry patches. Over a dirt road not yet warmed by the sun, or perhaps along the Duluth and Northeastern Railroad tracks, we would march with our pails through a world astir with the life of a new day. Chickadees sang lustily from every bush. Rabbits looped over fallen logs in the slashings. We might progress gaily for several miles before we reached the berry patch. Then we stowed our lunches in a shady spot and went to work, stripping the blueberries into our pails or picking the raspberries one by one from the fragrant bushes. There was always a spirit of competition among the berrypickers. It was a point of pride to pick more and faster than your companions; and so you worked industriously to fill your little lard pail quickly and empty it into a larger water bucket before anyone else.[5]

There were two natural types of berrypickers: one that settled down in a likely place and cleaned the bushes systematically before moving on, and one that flitted from patch to patch, always hoping to strike a bonanza. And there were the very small pickers, of course, who ate almost as many berries as they picked. But whatever our style, we kept at it through the hot August day until our big pail was full or the sun near the horizon. Then we started the long, trudging way back, much less exuberant than when we had set out. As we neared home, we emptied a small pail of big, plump berries on top of those in the large pail to make a nice, rounded heap that would look good and bring exclamations of praise from our mother.

As soon as the ground was dry in Johnson's pasture, we opened the baseball season. The pasture had a place that was clear of stumps and relatively level, and by removing any fresh cow patties that might have been deposited during the night, we had a fairly good baseball field.

Although we couldn't watch baseball on television or even listen to it on radio, we were all ardent fans. We followed the box scores and batting averages in the *Duluth Herald;* some of us could recite the averages of practically every player in both leagues. We all had our special heroes, too, and depending on what position you happened to be playing in Johnson's pasture, it wasn't too difficult to imagine yourself a Joe Tinker, Frank Chance, Ty Cobb, or Honus Wagner.

We played with whatever equipment our pooled resources could muster. A good deal of it was homemade. Until my Uncle Frank gave me a dollar baseball — a real "big league" ball with a stitched horsehide cover — we manufactured our own. We made them by winding ordinary store twine around a cork center. They started out pretty lopsided, but they gradually assumed the shape of a sphere and finally turned out to be passable baseballs — if you had never known any better.

In the matter of bats, we were lucky, Mush McGuire had a genuine Louisville Slugger, inherited from an older brother who had left for the harvest fields. Although some of us had gloves, there were never enough to go around, so outfielders often caught flies barehanded. I myself played behind the plate without chest protector or catcher's mask. After suffering a damaged nose from a foul tip, I fashioned a mask for myself from some heavy baling wire and strips of cloth for padding. It was not a success. The first ball to strike it made a deep dent across my already touchy nose, and I reverted to my barefaced style of catching.

Usually we chose up sides and played against each other, but sometimes we formed a team and took on another neighborhood nine. When this happened, we did not play in Johnson's pasture, but met our opponents on the baseball diamond in Pinehurst Park. Once we walked all the way to Carlton, a town six miles away, to play against another team of boys — then walked all the way back. We felt very professional and grown-up on these occasions.

Last summer I drove past a Little League ball park just as a shiny station wagon stopped and disgorged a tumble of small players in spick-and-span uniforms. I stopped, too, and watched while they scattered and began to shag fungoes. It took me back, as they say. But while I marveled at their beautiful playing field and splendid gear — including a real catcher's mask — I did not envy them for something I had missed in my own boyhood. In fact, I said to myself, "I think we had more fun maybe in Johnson's pasture."

With the advent of summer, the few people in our town who owned automobiles got them out of storage and began hopefully tuning them up for a spin in the country or just around the neighborhood. When I recall automobiles in Cloquet, it is a recollection veiled in clouds of dust on a summer's day.

Around the turn of the century, there were only about 120,000 cars in the whole United States (my *World Almanac* for 1907 tells me) and not many found their way to a small town like ours.[6] Those that did were apt to be broken-down castoffs from larger cities — like the one owned by Billy Horan's uncles.

Billy had two uncles who shared proprietorship in a vehicle whose name I do not remember. It seemed to tower on high wheels, had no top (at least, no remaining one), and you entered the back seat through a small door in the rear. Billy's uncles spent every evening after work tinkering with this car by lantern light. Neither of them knew anything about internal-combustion engines, but they doggedly pursued the hope that by taking things apart and putting them together again they could somehow make the automobile run. After tinkering all week, the test of their efforts came on Sunday. Billy's uncles, accompanied by all the children in the neighborhood and a few curious adults, would roll out the car and try to crank up the engine. Sometimes they succeeded and, after a series of frightening explosions, off they would lurch down the street. If you ran fast enough, you might catch up and climb through the rear door (always taking care not to step on the flywheel that projected through the floor) and enjoy a little joy ride. But never for long. Invariably the ungrateful engine conked out, and we who had cheered its short and noisy burst of life would silently help Billy's uncles push the auto back home.[7]

For a time the only man in Cloquet to own an automobile was Stokes Wilson, our mayor. Then a few others followed, among them the father of Hugo Schlenk, a friend of mine, who had a White Steamer, the latest model with acetylene headlights. One Sunday I was invited to go on a drive in the country with the family. We attained at one point, I remember very clearly, the reckless speed of thirty miles an hour.[8]

People who did own cars developed a fanatical enthusiasm for them. There were even popular songs about automobiles, like "In My Merry Oldsmobile," and one my Uncle Gus used to sing, beating time on the table with his beer mug:

> They say that the Rambler
> Ain't got any style,
> But she's style all the while,
> She's style all the while.

And there was a ditty with early antipollution overtones that went:

> Gasoline, gasoline —
> That's what makes the auto go,
> That's what smells
> Like hell, you know.

Some skeptics doubted the future of the self-propelled buggy, and it occurs to me with a sense of unbelief that I myself have uttered the derisive cry, "Get a horse!" But the cult of the auto was a steadily growing one, and in time even the nags of our town regarded their noisy rivals with nothing more than a wary indifference.

⋔

In our town a small boy's summer climaxed, you might say, with a hundred guns at sunrise. The signing of the Declaration of Independence was not so very far away in time. People were still living who could have seen and talked to its author himself.[9] So it was natural, perhaps, that the Glorious Fourth of July was celebrated with a noisy frontier exuberance very much to a boy's taste. The day opened with what the posters described as "a hundred gun salute at sunrise." I seem always to have been asleep at sunrise, and so never heard the salute. In time, I began to suspect that it was all a bit of hyperbole, and that there actually never was any.

The main event of the morning was the parade with the town band in uniform, a platoon of Spanish-American War veterans, the marshal of the day riding a white horse, floats representing local businesses, and along its whole route the cru-u-mp and sputter of firecrackers. In one respect, at least, our Fourth of July parade was different. It was the only one that had a Northern Lumber Company's float representing a logging camp cook shanty, with Joe Dugay, a famous camp cook, frying doughnuts at his camp range and tossing them to people along the way.

In the afternoon everybody drifted toward Pinehurst Park. There the young people sauntered about in pairs and groups, while their elders sat on the grass beside the lake and watched the birling. All the moppets ran races and all won prizes. The band played in the pavilion. There was a baseball game to which the crowds paid little attention, and a patriotic address by a state senator to which they paid even less. All day long the town resounded to the incessant explosions of firecrackers, small poppers that went off a whole string at a time, huge cannon crackers that could blow a washtub twenty feet high — or, as sometimes happened, tear off a man's arm. The air was heavy with the acrid smell of gunpowder.

If the weather was good, there might be a balloon ascension in Pinehurst Park.[10] The balloon was inflated by means of a wood fire built at one end of a trench that fed hot air into it. As the bag filled, mushroomed, and finally struggled to rise, it was held earth-bound by a gang of men clinging to its mooring ropes. When we kids volunteered to lend a hand on the ropes, we were roughly repulsed. There was a lot of shouting and excitement.

Suddenly, at some signal, everyone let go of the ropes and the balloon lurched skyward, dragging behind it a parachute and a man named Curley. Curley performed acrobatics on a trapeze high above the rooftops, growing smaller and smaller as the balloon drifted away. Finally, he cut his parachute loose, and we all held our breaths until it blossomed and Curley floated to earth. What made this performance awesome was not just the primitiveness of the apparatus, but the fact that between balloon ascensions Curley worked every day in one of the sawmills.

The Glorious Fourth wound up after dark with what the program posters called "a grand finale of fireworks and pyrotechnical displays." And this time the posters did not exaggerate. People sat beside the lake, watching the rockets as they burst and sprayed their blue, magenta, and cold green stars down from the high darkness and upward from the depths of the black water.

"A-a-a-a-h!" they all said together. "A-a-a-h," and "A-a-a-a-a-h," and "A-a-a-a-a-h!"

Then small crouching figures with torches ran about in the yellow smoke, and suddenly a huge American flag flared out of the darkness in sputtering color. And the Fourth was over.

Along with the public observance of the day, each family in Cloquet celebrated the Fourth in its own private and traditional fashion. With us the morning started by hanging out two large flags on the front porch, the staffs always nailed to the same two posts, with the nails in the same two holes. We always had a picnic on the Fourth, sometimes in the park, sometimes on our own lawn; my mother invariably made a meat loaf, with watermelon for dessert.

For my sisters and me the Fourth of July was marked by an event of towering dimensions: on that day, and that day only, my father gave each of us a silver dollar to spend as we pleased. And there was plenty to spend it on. In Pinehurst Park booths and stands mushroomed around the pavilion offering such good things to eat and drink as soda pop — lemon, orange, strawberry, sarsaparilla, and cream soda — hamburger and wiener sandwiches, and ice cream in the newly invented ice cream cones.[11] Various ladies' church societies operated bustling stands from which they dispensed cakes, brownies, homemade candies, doughnuts, and coffee. On this one day of the whole year, my sisters and I invariably bought a box of dark red Bing cherries.

Some of our money, of course, had to be saved for the pitchmen. These strangers came from out of town — we often wondered where — to set up their booths and shooting galleries. Their raucous chants sounded oddly foreign in our streets, almost like cries in an alien tongue. "The cane you ring is the cane you win, is the cane you carry away," one of them intoned. He held out three small wooden rings, challenging people to toss them at a glittering array of walking sticks. Nobody in Cloquet ever carried a cane, but on the Fourth many gladly paid their dime for three tries at ringing one and, as the pitchman said, carrying it away. It all looked very easy, but few succeeded. I could never resist squandering some of my money on these alluring games, but I cannot remember ever winning anything, except on one occasion three cigars. At the end of the day, I was always dead broke and feeling guilty about it, whereas my sisters still had a good share of their wealth intact in their little purses.

🌲

Band concerts were held irregularly during the summer whenever the musicians felt moved to go to Pinehurst Park and play. Although there was a pavilion in the park, the band usually preferred to form a circle and play in the open air, while people sat on the grass and listened.

The musicians were always surrounded by a ring of small boys, interested in watching them manipulate their instruments, and perhaps speculating idly on what would happen if a frog were dropped into Mr. Hansen's bass horn.

Moved by some primordial impulse, we were impelled to run around and around the circle of players as soon as the music started. When it stopped, we also stopped and dropped to the ground in mock exhaustion. When it started again, we were galvanized into action and resumed our dizzy racing around the band.

🌲

In our town picnics were a favorite summer recreation, and a popular picnic spot was Chub Lake. I do not know what has happened to Chub Lake. It has either dried up, I suppose, or become infested with summer cottages, motorboats, and water skiers. But it used to be a quiet little body of water, with a cool pine grove on one shore and a small sand beach nearby, and nothing noisier than kids splashing about to disturb the Sunday peace.

At least once during the summer, my father would hire a surrey from C. E. Johnson's Livery Stable ("New rigs, good horses") and we would drive the dusty but exciting six miles or so to Chub Lake. Sometimes my father would allow me to hold the reins. Quite a few people would be there on a fine Sunday, dressed in their best clothes, because people always dressed up for the Sabbath even on picnics. Perhaps the Odd

Fellows or the Sons of St. Olaf would be holding an outing, complete with a small band and a barrel of beer, and huge soda-fountain-size freezers of ice cream for the kids. It was all quite decorous and circumspect, the ladies twirling their parasols and gossiping or fussing with the refreshments, the men pitching horseshoes or just looking important and amused, the kids frolicking in the shallow water, young couples strolling off toward the pines. Something like what Renoir might have painted.

I am romanticizing, I suppose, but if I remember Chub Lake fondly, it is probably because its memory evokes a response that was natural and deep in the people of our town. There is as much water as land in northern Minnesota. Then, as now, an outing was apt to mean "a day at the lake," and for a small boy almost any summer afternoon was likely to lead him to water. Especially he would be drawn to the St. Louis River, the broad, quiet stream that flowed past our town and down to Lake Superior.

CHAPTER TEN

The Big, Wide Root Beer River

THE WATER of the St. Louis River is clear but deep brown in color. Where it foams over boulders, as it does at the dalles, it had for us, as I am sure it has for children today, the exact appearance of a cataract of root beer.

If you take a canoe and paddle upstream until you reach the great oxbow bend near Floodwood, you will come to a place where you might lift out your canoe and carry it to the headwaters of the Mississippi.[1] In the old days that is just what many an Indian hunter and fur trader did, and the *Rivière St. Louis* became a famous highway of the French *voyageurs*. Knife Falls, by which name Cloquet was first known, was so called because the canoemen often bruised and cut their moccasined feet on the sharp rocks of the portage there. If you listen closely on a dark night, it is said, you can still hear their ghostly *sacrés!* above the rapids.

But the *voyageurs* and the colorful past of the *Rivière St. Louis* had long been forgotten by the people of Cloquet. In the early 1900s small boys knew it only as a fascinating call to adventure on a hazy summer day.

Sometimes, when you were coming home from hunting squirrels or picking blueberries along the north bank of the river, you would see rivermen rolling logs. It was their sport, just as turkey shoots were with the frontiersmen and steer roping with western cowboys. There was nobody better at birling — which is the proper name of the sport — than Cloquet rivermen. Will Delyea, who lived on our street, was the best of them all; he became the champion birler of the whole world.[2]

"As easy as rolling off a log," people say — or, at any rate, they used to. This saying tells you why birling was a sport: it was the sport of standing on a log with another man and trying to roll him into the water. If you have ever tried to stand on a free-rolling log, you might suppose that such a contest would not last very long. But a pair of good birlers might "cuff the bubbles" for hours until one of them collapsed from sheer exhaustion.

We loved to sit on the grassy bank of the St. Louis and watch the rivermen birl. Standing on opposite ends of a large log, two of them would begin turning it treadmill-fashion with the sharp steel calks in their driving boots Sometimes, with their eyes on each other's feet, they would turn the log slowly and craftily, like boxers sparring for an opening . . . waiting for the split second of carelessness when a sudden burst of speed might catch one of them off balance and end the contest with an unexpected and ignominious splash. Or with the log spinning briskly, one of the birlers might leap into the air, turning catlike. Landing with his calks driven deeply into the log, he could thus bring it to a sudden and complete stop. The defense against this maneuver was to perform the same trick simultaneously. Both birlers would then be left facing each other, backs bent and arms hanging, like two toms on a back fence.

Some birling contests were terminated by such tactics, but usually they ended with one man falling off the log simply because he was too exhausted to stay on it. You could always tell when the end was near. The stronger of the birlers, sensing the other's failing strength, would turn the log faster and faster until it disappeared almost completely beneath the water, and the men seemed to be running madly side by side on a narrow strip of foam. The weaker, his leg muscles striving desperately to meet the other's pace, would fall farther and farther back, until at last, with outflung arms, he was thrown on his back into the water.

On the Fourth of July there were always birling contests in Pinehurst Park, and it was exciting to watch them, with the band playing "Waltz Me Around Again, Willie," and a big crowd cheering the winners. But it was even better to happen on the rivermen rolling logs on the St. Louis, with their fellow workers watching from the deck of the wanigan. For some reason, sounds seem to come across water with a special clarity, and I can still hear with startling immediacy the wild guffaws of the rivermen whenever a birler, with pumping legs and flailing arms, plunged into the placid brown water of the river.

You could hardly call it whiling away a summer's day, but there was a diversion somewhat related to birling that a boy sometimes turned to when nothing else offered itself. We called it running logs.

The St. Louis, as you know, was jammed from bank to bank with sawlogs during the summer, with only occasional small patches of water visible. The logs were of all sizes, ranging from small "sticks" to huge logs three or four feet across the butt end. They drifted together side by side in clusters, and the sport of running logs consisted in skipping across a cluster of small logs to the safety of a big one. You skipped as fast and lightly as you could across the small logs (which immediately sank beneath you) to the haven of a big, solid one that would support your weight. Then you looked around for another "grandpa."

Once you left shore you were committed to continuing until you reached the far bank. You were "chicken" if you turned back. Running logs was a pastime not without hazard. A small log might sink under you too quickly, or you could slip on a piece of loose bark. It was easy to find yourself in the water, and you were lucky if you did not strike your head on a log on the way down and knock yourself out, or maybe come up under a close-packed cluster of logs. It was, in fact, a foolhardy sport rigidly interdicted by our parents — which was one of its attractions, I suppose, to a boy with nothing much to do on a long, hot day.

There was a sort of legend in our town about a Finnish mother whose little son had drowned while running logs on the river. Every night, it was said, workers in the Northern Lumber Company mill could see her walking along the banks of the St. Louis, calling for this little boy who had been a long time dead.

♠

Occasionally we would range as far up the river as the boomhouse, three miles from town. Here logs from the camps were sorted according to their "company marks" for the different mills down river.[3] The sorting crews who pushed the logs with their long limber pike poles into the proper "pens" took their meals and were generally lodged in the boomhouse, a low frame structure on the riverside near the sorting booms.

The boomhouse cook was Joe Dugay, a jovial French Canadian whose skill at the camp range was legendary. Like all good cooks, Joe loved to see people eat, and he was generous enough to include among people any small boy who "happened" to drop by for a visit. His tables were always set, and a couple of young squirrel hunters or nutters always welcome. In an atmosphere fragrant with the blended aromas of kitchen and river, Joe would urge you to "deeg in" and the only problem was where to begin. For never, I suppose, were the eyes of small boys famished from a three-mile hike dazzled by a more remarkable array of goodies.

Of fresh breads, still warm from the oven, there were more than I can remember. Among them were thick slices of soft and creamy white bread, coffeecake, sugared rolls, big wheels of hardtack (which none of us ever touched), and dark, moist rye loaves. Of pies, there would be raisin, prune, apple, peach, blueberry, lemon (made with lemon extract), and "larrigan" or "shoepack" pie (made with nobody could guess what). There were also deep tin dishes heaped with doughnuts, crullers, and cookies (white and dark) as big as saucers. All this and much more spread out before our hungry eyes, and Joe Dugay bellowing, "Deeg in! W'at's de matter wid you fellers — you got no appe*tite?* Deeg in!"

When I was young, an old man once said to me, "When I look back on all the people I knew as a child, it seems to me I remember best those who fed me." Like, for instance, Joe Dugay.

🌲

There were two places where a boy could swim. The one across the river from the Johnson-Wentworth mill was a small bay in the St. Louis under some tall elm trees. It had the advantage of privacy. You could swim there in a natural state without fear of any female berrypickers catching you drying off on the grassy bank. The disadvantage was the long walk home, mostly uphill, in the weakened state induced by hunger and a long afternoon in the tepid water of the St. Louis. Sometimes it seemed you would never make it to the kitchen and a thick slice of bread covered with corn syrup.

The sand bar, a sandy shallow in the middle of the river, was our other, and more popular, swimming hole. Completely hemmed in by booms, it provided a clear space, free of logs, in which rivermen could practice birling and boys could swim. It was the domain of Jonas Delyea, a tall, mustached riverman who was boom boss.[4] His headquarters were the wanigan, a sort of shanty on a log raft. Jonas was a strict moralist and made us wear swimming trunks, very skimpy affairs, always patterned in narrow horizontal stripes and secured around the waist by a drawstring. They cost twenty cents.

Jonas Delyea was the father of Will Delyea, whom I have mentioned as the champion birler of the world, and he was very good on the logs himself. It was said he could waltz across a chocolate cake in his driving boots without scratching the frosting. He was fond of youngsters and let us paddle about in a dugout canoe tied to the wanigan. Sometimes he would give us lessons in birling.

Nobody gave us lessons in swimming, however. We just paddled happily about dog fashion or maybe tried the breast stroke as we grew older. Sometimes a swimmer would yell, "Wanna see the moon?" and duck under water, holding his nose while briefly exposing his bottom. But this trick lost its point when, at Jonas' insistence, it had to be performed in swimming trunks.

Except for the distant boomhouse, there was not another building in sight of the sand bar. There was only the grassy bank with clumps of tall elm trees along the opposite side of the river. And there were no sounds at all, except the remote hum of the sawmills and the shouts of small water animals called boys. No shrieking girls, no life guards, no parked cars or hot dog stands, and best of all, no adults except Jonas and a few rivermen.

⚐

If there was even a small fly in the ointment of those idyllic summer days, it probably was "Old Mac." His real name was John McSweeney, and he was Cloquet's chief of police.[5] In fact, he was the entire police force. Old Mac was not really old; with his grizzled mustache he only seemed so to small boys. He wore no uniform, carried no arms, but his authority was well advertised by a resplendent badge, a worn-looking blackjack protruding from his hip pocket, and a powerful physique. He was well able (as I myself once witnessed) to handle two drunken lumberjacks single-handed, yet mobile enough to track a young criminal to the ends of the earth, or at any rate to the ends of Cloquet.

Old Mac owed his extraordinary mobility to his bicycle. He was never seen without it, and people got so used to seeing Old Mac and his bicycle together that they sometimes failed to recognize him afoot. With his bike he covered the whole town so swiftly that you could never be sure he wouldn't appear suddenly and silently at the scene of a crime. When he did apprehend you in some breach of the law such as raiding Mr. McGuire's crabapple tree, or carrying a concealed slingshot, or playing under the street light after curfew, Old Mac would let you quake for a while, then he would deliver a lecture. It was always the same lecture, and it always ended with the same stern warning: "Well, I'll let ye go this once't, but next time I'll run ye in."

Old Mac instilled in us a deep respect for — or perhaps it was a fear of — the law, but he never really ran any of us in. And, despite the terror he struck in our young hearts, I do not think that any of us remembered him unkindly.

CHAPTER ELEVEN

Summer Visitors

NOT MANY PEOPLE came to Cloquet. Even in summer our town was almost as isolated as a logging camp in the deep woods. Nobody except settlers in the cutover ever came over the dirt roads leading into town. Few travelers climbed down from "Gilbert's train" except drummers from the Twin Cities or people visiting relatives. Some of the older girls found something — the drummers, no doubt — interesting enough to draw them to the station at traintime. But there was nothing their younger brothers could find very fascinating in a slick-looking salesman for shoes or ladies' wear. Yet there were a few who came — some in mysterious ways — that one would not forget. Some who brought with them an intimation of wonders beyond our hills, and left behind them a vague unrest in our young hearts.

Once a Tom show visited Cloquet and performed the play of *Uncle Tom's Cabin* in the opera house.[1] The occasion was preceded by a city-looking stranger with a mouth full of tacks which he fed through his lips to a magnetic hammer to nail up colored posters announcing the coming show.

I was always sorry that I never saw Eliza crossing the ice, her eyes wild and her hair streaming, with her baby in her arms and the bloodhounds pursuing her, as the posters showed it. But we who did not have the price of admission to the show could at least watch the parade on the afternoon before the performance. The actors marched in Old South costumes, with a small band of blackface musicians, and Simon Legree cracking his whip as he strode down Main Street behind a

106

cringing Uncle Tom. We pitied Uncle Tom, of course, but really we had eyes only for Little Eva.

A golden-haired, blue-eyed vision in snowy dimity, she rode in a pony cart drawn by a tiny Shetland, distributing sad, sweet smiles along the route of parade — and once, I was quite sure, she smiled at me. As soon as her pony cart had passed, we raced down the street ahead of the parade, so as to see her when she went by again.

I have no wish to diminish the charms of the young ladies of Cloquet, many of which were not to be taken lightly. But which of them, after all, could hope to compete with Little Eva — she of the azure eyes, and golden curls, and sad, sweet smile?

🌲

We may not have had much fresh fruit in our town, but once every summer we had plenty of watermelons — a whole freight car full of them, straight from the melon patches of the South.

A good many people came down to the railroad siding to watch the unloading, which was performed by several black men. Some came, no doubt, because they had nothing better to do, and some out of curiosity. Others were prepared to buy a big, ripe melon for a nickel or a dime. But to the lesser of us, the black men were the main attraction, even more fascinating than the sight of so many melons. For except when a circus or minstrel show came to town, Negroes were almost unknown in Cloquet, and everyone watched these black men with amused interest.

"H'yah!" they shouted, clowning it up as they tossed the melons out of the dark interior of the freight car in a sort of bucket line. "H'yah!" Their teeth flashed in their dark, shiny faces, and moppets peered at them a little fearfully from behind the legs of parents. "H'yah — hunh!" The blacks knew they were providing entertainment; they laughed and shouted and imparted an air of fiesta to the unloading of the melons.

Occasionally one of them would misjudge his catch, and a

melon would fly into delicious red and green fragments on the siding. Then the blacks would pause and grin at the ensuing scramble of small boys; and it was not hard to see that sometime the melons slipped through their hands rather easily.

♠

On one special day of the year, our parents allowed us to set the alarm clock at four o'clock in the morning and steal from the house before anyone else was awake. That was the day the Walter L. Main shows came to town.[2]

It would still be dark when we arrived at the railroad siding where the circus was unloading from flatcars. Flaring gasoline torches cast wild shadows over a scene of murky chaos; shouting roustabouts ducking in and out of the lighted areas; strange animal cries and grunts; the monstrous forms of elephants looming in the darkness, sometimes so near that we scattered in panic; cages and ornate wagons lumbering down the ramps from flatcars; a mob of people from another world milling about in the predawn half-light.

Hardly less spectacular than the unloading was the breathtaking speed with which the "big top" blossomed on the Company's horse pasture west of town. We watched bug-eyed as long lines of roustabouts pulled on ropes with rhythmic shouts, and the great spread of canvas rose slowly from the ground to the top of the tall poles; at the big black men, stripped to the waist, beating a tattoo with alternate strokes of their sledge hammers on the stakes that would hold the tent securely to the ground; at the swift erection of a whole street of gaudy side-show booths and refreshment stands. It all engendered a mounting excitement that caused some boys to talk about joining the circus, but nobody in our town ever did.

Most boys sought jobs that would gain them "free" admission to the circus; but others preferred to sneak, if they could, under the canvas of the big top. Traditionally, boys earned their way into the circus by watering the elephants. I was never privileged to perform this glamorous chore; but I did attain a certain prominence among my agemates one year by riding a small camel in the parade, with a red fez on my head.

Among other summer visitors to Cloquet were the horse traders, dusty, leathery men in high-heeled boots and big hats, who unloaded western ponies from cattle cars and auctioned them off at the railroad siding. More frequent were the visits of the medicine men, selling their nostrums by the light of gasoline flares, with banjo music and sly jokes to lure the customers up nearer the show. One of them holds aloft two bottles (for the price of one) of his Great Sioux Indian remedy for rheumatism and most other aches and pains. He points sternly at his audience and demands, "Have any of you ever seen a Sioux Indian limping down Main Street?" I remember sensing some flaw in his logic, for all our Indians were Chippewas.

Then, of course, there were the gypsies, but I am sorry I cannot tell you very much about them. There was a flat, grassy meadow on the far side of the river, where they made their encampment. Once we crept near enough by a circuitous route to spy on them from a hazel thicket. But when some dogs began barking and a large, swarthy man seemed to be coming toward us, we scurried out of there.

The gypsies, our parents warned us, besides stealing horses were known to have stolen children, but we wondered why the gypsies or anyone else would want to steal us. As we saw them going about Cloquet, the men with their silver ornaments and the women in their brightly colored dresses, they did not seem especially sinister, only strange and exciting.

For a little while the streets and stores of Cloquet echoed with the strident laughter of the black-eyed women, who, although strangers and suspected ones at that, swung their skirts and jingled their bravery as if they owned the town. But the gypsies did not remain long in their encampment on the river. After a few days Old Mac ordered them to move along, and they departed in their high, gaily painted wagons as quietly and mysteriously as they had come. Before, we had wondered where they had come from; now we wondered where they had gone.

🌲

We also had summer visitors from other worlds. One was a ghost that frequented the Indian graveyard on the Fond du Lac Reservation. A lot of people went up to see it, and returned to tell about a pale light that wandered among the little wooden houses that stood over the Chippewa graves. Some professors were brought up from the University of Minnesota to take a look at the strange lights, but they pronounced them nothing but marsh gas. This, however, did not convince a lot of people that they had not seen a real ghost.

I myself did not observe the graveyard spook, but I did see one — or at least its picture — in a family portrait that Ole Olson took.[3] Not many people owned cameras in those days, so if you wanted your picture taken, you had to go to a professional photographer like Ole; and he would take it from under a black cloth draped over his head. It was quite an event to have your picture taken, and a family portrait was especially important.

There was a millworker in Cloquet whose wife had longed to have a picture taken of their large, fine family. The project was always delayed, however, until, at last, the mother died. Then the father did go to Ole's studio and have a family portrait taken of himself and his children. When Ole developed the plates, there was the mother, standing behind the others.

Ole displayed an enlarged print in the window of his studio; and sure enough, it showed a distinct face and figure that, her friends said, looked just like the dead woman's. This, I suppose, was the most remarkable thing that happened in our town all that summer.

CHAPTER TWELVE

That Was Timber!

THEN the yellow harvest moon turned red in the smoke of distant brush fires, wavering V's of mallards drifted across the sky, and suddenly one morning the sloping roofs of Cloquet glittered with hoar frost. Fall had arrived again.

Thus the seasons turned on the St. Louis, and so my memories of a boy's year follow the pattern of their turning. It was a succession as ordered and sure as the flight of wild ducks southward in the fall and their homing in the spring: the mills falling silent with the freeze-up, the men leaving for the woods, their return when the camps broke in spring, the mills getting up steam for the summer run . . . It was all as natural and inevitable to the people of our town as the seasons of planting, growing, and harvesting are to farmers. And it would go on forever . . .

But all was not well, really, and some of the people of Cloquet seemed to have sensed this without actually admitting it to one another. As early as 1904 there was a lot of talk in our town about the great stands of white pine in Idaho; as if impelled by some ancient instinct, a good many men suddenly decided to go west and "have a look at the country." Their fathers and forefathers had followed the pine across half a continent and, whether or not they knew it, the old urge was still in their blood.

My father was one of those who joined this exodus. When he returned, he had marvelous stories to tell about a little town in Idaho called Coeur d'Alene. He described it so often and so minutely that I came to visualize it very clearly as a kind of Happy Valley of verdant fields and flowering or-

chards, ringed by snow-capped mountains. I have never seen
Coeur d'Alene and I hope I never shall, lest that lovely vision
of my boyhood be destroyed.[1]

For all its charms, my father did not return to Coeur
d'Alene. But quite a few families from our town did go west,
the vanguard of the last trek in the long migration of rivermen and shanty boys from the Penobscot to the giant fir
forests of the Pacific Coast.

When, as a youth, I myself "went up in the woods" and
spent a winter in Netser's camp on Pequayan Lake, the
twilight of logging in northern Minnesota had deepened almost to night. Ed Netser was one of the last great camp bosses
of his era, and he ran his operation in the classic horse-
logging tradition. With a hundred men, we cut over seven
million feet of pine that winter, landed it on Pequayan Lake,
and drove it down the St. Louis without benefit of an ounce of
steam. In Netser's camp on Pequayan you might have thought
yourself in the great old days of logging, in the golden
time when the pine would go on forever.

Yet the end was near. It came suddenly, preceded by a
firestorm of terror and destruction. In the month of October,
1918, as if in retribution for the carnage wrought by the
logger's ax, the vast cutover encircling Cloquet burst into
flame, and a great conflagration wiped out almost every ves-
tige of human habitation in our town.[2] After the National
Guard had departed, a thousand pitiful little shacks of raw
wood mushroomed on the site of Cloquet. People were re-
turning to the ashes, perhaps because they had nowhere else
to go — because they wanted to be where the pine was.

But it took only a few years to cut the last of the pine.
Almost overnight, it seemed, none at all was left. The logging
camps were suddenly empty and silent, the St. Louis as free of
logs as when the *voyageurs* plied it. And not another foot of
lumber was ever cut in "The White Pine Capital of the
World."

Then new industries moved in. Farmers brought loads of
the despised "popple" and spruce for the manufacture of
wallboard, toothpicks, and kitchen matches. Many an old-
time lumberjack must have turned in his grave, but the people of Cloquet cheerfully told one another that it would be a

better town than ever. And perhaps they were right. Perhaps Cloquet really is a better town without its great sawmills, its miles of sweet-smelling lumber in stately piles along the river, its inexhaustible supply of white pine logs in the wide, slow-flowing St. Louis. But I am glad that I knew it as it used to be.

I am thankful that all my memories of Cloquet are as it was before the pine was gone. And that the voice I still hear from that long-vanished past is old Tom Mogan's: "By God, Mike, that was timber!" For that was a good time, a good place, for a boy to grow up in — for an old man to remember.

Reference Notes

Chapter 1 — WONDERS AND MARVELS, 1906 — pages 1 to 7

[1] Mr. O'Meara may be a bit off in his timing here. Thomas Mogan was a logging camp boss for the Northern Lumber Company. The *Pine Knot* of September 2, 1905, reported that "Thomas Mogan who has been ill at St. Mary's hospital in Duluth for some time returned to the city Wednesday, much improved in health." Ed.

[2] *World Almanac and Encyclopedia, 1907,* 142, 144, 262, 281 (New York, 1906).

[3] The generally accepted explanation is that the town took its name from the principal tributary of the St. Louis River, which appears as the Cloquet River on Joseph N. Nicollet's 1843 map. How the river got its name is unknown. One theory suggests that it was named for 19th-century French scientists Hippolyte and Jules Cloquet. See Warren Upham, *Minnesota Geographic Names: Their Origin and Historic Significance,* 74 (St. Paul, 1969); *The White Pine,* 4 (Cloquet, 1936), the Cloquet High School yearbook. Ed.

[4] There were five mills in Cloquet in 1906, at least one of which was powered by water. Two were operated by the Cloquet Lumber Company, two by the Northern Lumber Company, and one by the Johnson-Wentworth Company. By 1906 all three firms were owned by the Weyerhaeusers. See Ralph W. Hidy, Frank E. Hill, and Allan Nevins, *Timber and Men: The Weyerhaeuser Story,* 189 (New York, 1963); "White Pine's Journey From Minnesota Forests," in *American Lumberman,* August 3, 1907, p. 72. Ed.

[5] Shawtown and Nelsontown were named for millowners Charles N. Nelson of the Charles N. Nelson Lumber Company and George S. Shaw of the Cloquet Lumber Company. For additional data on the various sections which sprang up after Cloquet was platted in 1883, see Lillian Eilers, "Cloquet — The Wood City," in *Carlton County Centennial Program, 1857–1957,* [14] (Cloquet, 1957); Matt Pelkonen, "Cloquet on Parade," 26, a photocopy of a typescript in the Minnesota Historical Society's library. Mr. O'Meara wrote the editor on July 2, 1974: "I remember my father telling me that George S. Shaw lived and died over his company store." The two company stores operated by the Cloquet and Northern companies were consolidated in 1907. Hidy, *et al., Timber and Men,* 193. Ed.

115

[6] Isaac Goldberg, *The Wonder of Words: An Introduction to Language for Everyman,* 152 (New York, 1938).

[7] For the origins of "Protestant Boys," see Redfern Mason, *The Song Lore of Ireland,* 255 (New York, 1910). Ed.

Chapter 2 — THEY FOLLOWED THE PINE — pages 8 to 16

[1] Father Simon Lampe, a Benedictine priest from St. John's Abbey at Collegeville, served the Fond du Lac mission from 1905 until 1923. He died in 1940 at Red Lake. See Sister Bernard Coleman, *Where the Water Stops (Fond du Lac Reservation),* 7 (Duluth, 1967); *Bemidji Daily Pioneer,* June 11, 1937; *The Oblate,* 14 : 96 (December, 1940), a periodical issued by St. John's. Ed.

[2] On the baseball career of Will Cadreau, "better known as 'Neche,'" see *Pine Knot,* May 23, 1908, October 8, 1910. Ed.

[3] *Pine Knot,* July 15, 1905, reported that "The La Prairie brothers are beyond question the best log rollers in this section." Ed.

[4] Although the fur traders often crossed the portage that became the site of Knife Falls in 1878–79, the loggers who built the mills and the town were the first permanent settlers on what had been Indian lands. See Stewart Holbrook, *Holy Old Mackinaw: A Natural History of the American Lumberjack,* 76–78 (New York, 1956).

[5] *Pine Knot,* February 16, 1907, reported that its representative "was the guest of John Long Tuesday at his camp 1 . . . about five miles from Stroud. Mr. Long has a five-year contract in this vicinity with the Northern Lumber company and this is his second winter's work. . . . It is expected that when spring opens, between eight and nine million feet of logs will have been landed on Bug Creek, scattered up and down that stream for a distance of three miles. The logs will be driven from Bug Creek into the Whiteface and thence into the St. Louis." For more information on Long, who later became mayor of Cloquet, see Pelkonen, "Cloquet on Parade," 33. Ed.

[6] One version of this song appears in Carl Sandburg, *The American Songbag,* 360 (New York, 1927), under the title "Jerry, Go An' Ile That Car." It begins: "Come all ye railroad section men / An listen to my song / It is of Larry O'Sullivan / Who now is dead and gone." Ed.

[7] St. Mary's Hospital in Duluth, established in 1898 by the Benedictine sisters, "sold tickets to the men in the lumber industry covering the cost of their hospital and medical care should they be sick or injured. The price of the tickets varied somewhat, but was in the neighborhood of $12 per year." Richard Bardon, "The Background of Medical History for Northeastern Minnesota and the Lake Superior Region," in *Minnesota Medicine,* 21 : 122 (February, 1938). See also *Pine Knot,* January 18, 1908. Ed.

[8] There is much controversy about whether the Paul Bunyan stories are authentic folk legends of the lumbering era, or whether they are the later creations of writers and advertising men. The first printed reference to Paul is in James MacGillivray, "The Round River Drive," in the *Detroit News-Tribune* of July 24, 1910. Credit for popularization of the Paul Bunyan legend with certain additions of his own must go on to W. B. Laughead, who wrote in 1914 the first of a series of advertising pamphlets for the Red River Lumber

Company entitled *Introducing Mr. Paul Bunyan of Westwood, Cal.* For additional information, see Daniel G. Hoffman, *Paul Bunyan: Last of the Frontier Demigods* (Philadelphia, 1952). Ed.

[9] A roster for Alexander Henry's Red River brigade, 1800–01, may be found in Elliott Coues, ed., *New Light on the Early History of the Greater Northwest*, 1 : 49–52(New York, 1897).

[10] The church burned on September 18, 1908. See Patrick J. Lydon, "Notes on the History of the Diocese of Duluth," in *Acta et Dicta*, 5 : 270 (July, 1918). Ed.

[11] For additional information on Carl Bruno and his family, see Pelkonen, "Cloquet on Parade," 50. Ed.

[12] On this group, variously referred to as the "Viking Singing Society," the "Viking Choir," and the "Viking Male Chorus," see *Pine Knot*, June 6, July 25, 1908, May 15, 1909, June 25, 1910. Ed.

[13] For additional information on Edmund "Eddie" Kuitu and his family, see Pelkonen, "Cloquet on Parade," 57. Ed.

[14] John M. Crawford, trans., *The Kalevala: The Epic Poem of Finland*, 1 : 63 (New York, 1888). At the time this edition was published, much of the Kalevala had only recently been written down from orally preserved Finnish traditions.

[15] According to the 1900 population census, Cloquet had a total of 3,072 people, 1,368 of whom were foreign born. See *Twelfth Census of the United States, 1900*, 1 : 624 (Washington, D.C., 1901). Ed.

Chapter 3 — AND SO DID WE — pages 17 to 25

[1] For Michael O'Meara's obituary, see *Pine Knot*, September 10, 1948. Ed.

[2] On the 33-year Donnelly depredations which began in 1847, see Thomas P. Kelley, *The Black Donnellys*, [7] (Toronto, 1954).

[3] Miss May J. Wolfe, Mr. O'Meara's mother, is listed as a milliner in Cloquet in 1894–95, and Wolfe & Fornance are listed in 1896–97. *Minnesota, North and South Dakota and Montana Gazetteer and Business Directory, 1894–95*, 238; *1896–97*, 250 (St. Paul, 1894, 1896), hereafter cited as *Gazetteer*. Ed.

[4] A number of families, including that of Andrew Wolfe, are said to have moved together from Louisville, Kentucky, to Rosewood Landing, Harrison County, Indiana, and from there to Chippewa County, Minnesota. Andrew is reported to have settled in Rosewood Township, Chippewa County, about 1869. He became treasurer of the township in 1871 and county commissioner in 1876. He died only a few weeks after assuming the latter office in 1876. Lycurgus R. Moyer and O. G. Dale, *History of Chippewa and Lac qui Parle Counties*, 1 : 190, 206; 2 : 84 (Indianapolis, 1916). Ed.

[5] The firm of Kelly & Moses, composed of William Kelly and David Moses, is listed as operating a general store and undertaking establishment at 112 Avenue C in *Gazetteer, 1906–1907*, 307. On Moses, see also Pelkonen, "Cloquet on Parade," 21. Ed.

[6] Ellen Fornance is listed as a widow residing at 4116 Bryant Avenue South, Minneapolis, from 1912 to 1919. See *Davison's Minneapolis City Directory, 1912*, 667; *1913*, 654; *1914*, 709; *1915*, 698; *1916*, 733; *1917*, 746; *1918*, 620; *1919*, 640. J. Alwin Fesenbeck is listed as an attorney at law in Cloquet with

"prompt attention to collections" at 204 Arch Street. *Gazetteer, 1906–1907*, 306. Ed.

[7] Miss Hillbrand died in 1972. See *St. Paul Dispatch*, February 23, 1972, p. 67. Among her published works are *Our Minnesota: The Geography and History of Our State*, written with James W. Clark (Syracuse, N.Y., 1964), and *The Norwegians in Minnesota* (Minneapolis, 1967). Ed.

[8] Carl E. Johnson is listed as being in the livery and fuel business at 126 Avenue C. *Gazetteer, 1906–1907*, 307. Ed.

[9] For an illustrated account of these events, see Kenneth Carley, *The Sioux Uprising of 1862* (St. Paul, 1961). Ed.

[10] On these songs, which were published in 1906 and 1907, see Sigmund Spaeth, *A History of Popular Music in America*, 275, 356, 357 (New York, 1948). Ed.

[11] "Coax Me," composed in 1904, was sung very naughtily by Anna Held, a famous French-American singer and actress at the turn of the century who was later known chiefly for her enticing French accent, her rolling eyes, and her milk baths. She was married to Florenz Ziegfeld, Jr., a well-known theatrical producer.

Chapter 4 — SOMETHING OVER OUR HEADS pages 26 to 34

[1] The forest fire that destroyed Cloquet occurred on October 12, 1918. For full accounts of it, see Stewart H. Holbrook, *Burning an Empire*, 31–45 (New York, 1943); Pelkonen, "Cloquet on Parade," 62–66. Ed.

[2] *Pine Knot*, May 27, 1905, reported: "The lumber is on the ground for M. O'Mara's [*sic*] new residence on Third Street. It will be built by Contractor Gorham." Ed.

[3] The contest in which the O'Mearas won the third prize of $25.00 took place in the summer and fall of 1906. See *Pine Knot*, April 21, May 5, November 3, 1906. Ed.

[4] Ouida was the pen name of Marie Louise de la Ramée, an English author of romances and children's stories who died in 1908. Ed.

[5] *The Farmer's Guide* recalled by Mr. O'Meara may have been a book entitled *The Farmer's Guide and Western Agriculturist*, which was first published by the Hamilton County Agricultural Society at Cincinnati, Ohio, in 1832. The poem quoted, entitled "Which Shall It Be?" by Ethel Lynn Beers, appears in Henry T. Coates, ed., *The Fireside Encyclopedia of Poetry*, 33 (Philadelphia, 1878). "Over the Hill to the Poor-house" by Will Carleton was first published in *Harper's Weekly*, June 17, 1871. Ed.

[6] Pierce, *The People's Common Sense Medical Adviser*, viii (Chicago, 1895), the 67th edition of this popular volume. Ed.

Chapter 5 — DIGGING IN — pages 35 to 49

[1] Peter F. Moody, barber, operated a shop at 201 Arch Street. *Gazetteer, 1906–1907*, 307. Ed.

[2] The small lake is probably located in section 6 in northwestern Knife Falls Township, Carlton County, about six miles from Cloquet. It remains unnamed today. Ed.

[3] See Frank G. Menke, *The Encyclopedia of Sports*, 360 (New York, 1953). Ed.

[4] See Charles M. Wilson, *The Magnificent Scufflers*, 81 (Brattleboro, Vt., 1959). On the boxers in the paragraph below, see *World Almanac and Encyclopedia, 1907*, 281 (New York, 1906); *Nat Fleisher's All-Time Ring Record Book*, 45, 186, 281, 319 (Norwalk, Conn., 1943). Ed.

[5] Joseph Loisel was a large rotund man weighing 256 pounds, whose hardware store was located at 111 Avenue C. He also served as Cloquet city clerk. There are numerous good-humored references to his weight in the *Pine Knot*, January 21, 1905, February 24, 1906, July 25, 1907. See also *Gazetteer, 1906–1907*, 307. Ed.

[6] According to *Gazetteer, 1906–1907*, 308, B. J. Summerfield operated several clothing and drygoods stores in Cloquet. For additional information on his career, see *Pine Knot*, March 14, 1908. Ed.

[7] McGilvray grew up to become Cloquet's city assessor. See Pelkonen, "Cloquet on Parade," 41. Ed.

Chapter 6 — THE SNOWS CAME — pages 50 to 62

[1] These birds are also known as snow buntings. Ed.

[2] Frederick A. Grunig operated two meat markets in Cloquet at 128 Avenue C and 1065 Cloquet Avenue; *Gazetteer, 1906–1907*, 306. Ed.

[3] Mr. O'Meara wrote the editor in July, 1974: "Incidentally John White was widely known as Johnny Bull, since he was a native-born Englishman, a rare thing in Cloquet, and had a very John Bull look about him. He drove a spirited pinto stallion."White and his wife returned to England for three months during the winter of 1903–04, according to the *Pine Knot*, December 12, 1903. Ed.

[4] Grapefruit (*Citrus paradisi*) was first described in the West Indies in 1750, was introduced to Florida by the Spanish, and was first commercially grown there about 1880. It had been suspected as early as the 1890s that such diseases as scurvy and beriberi were caused by dietary deficiencies, but it was not until 1912 that the word "vitamin" was coined by Casimir Funk. The first vitamin to be chemically pinpointed was vitamin A in 1913. Ed.

[5] The helpful librarians at the Minneapolis Public Library found a 1953 Burl Ives version of the song recalled by Mr. O'Meara under the title "My Momma Told Me," which begins "My Momma told me that she would buy me a rubber dolly if I were good" followed by the portion quoted. Ed.

[6] Patrick Ronan is listed as a confectioner in business at 127 Avenue A. *Gazetteer, 1906–1907*, 307. Ed.

Chapter 7 — DEEP WINTER — pages 63 to 75

[1] Swan had broken the moose to harness while very young, and it was his custom to drive through town on a winter day, waving bibulous greetings to

the citizenry. But the state finally took his moose away from him and put them in the St. Paul zoo. At least, that is the way I heard it.

[2] According to the *Pine Knot*, January 21, 1905, "Coasting on Chestnut street is again a popular pastime, the weather being especially favorable for this sport." The newspaper described the toboggan slide that was built in Pinehurst Park in 1907 in its issues of December 7, 14, 21, 1907. Ed.

[3] I have recently found a letter I wrote to my Aunt Dell in 1906 that explains why: I had been sick.

[4] Luther A. Freeman, jeweler and watchmaker, is listed as having a store at 210 Arch Street. *Gazetteer, 1906–1907,* 306. Ed.

[5] Nelson's Opera House was located at the corner of Arch Street and Avenue B. *Gazetteer, 1906–1907,* 307. Ed.

[6] The drugstore of George H. Kopp and Emil J. Proulx operated at 214 Arch Street. *Gazetteer, 1906–1907,* 307. Ed.

[7] The grocery store of Oscar A. Knitu and John A. Mattinen was located at 127 Avenue A, according to *Gazetteer, 1906–1907,* 307. The *Pine Knot,* January 2, 1904, identifies George Gilbert as the conductor on the Northern Pacific running between Cloquet and Duluth. Ed.

[8] There is a note in the *Pine Knot,* May 5, 1906, saying that a group of people from Cloquet took the train to Duluth to see Sarah Bernhardt in a performance of *Camille,* but Mr. O'Meara seems to have remembered her on a later tour. Or, he says, the *Pine Knot* may have erred. Ed.

[9] The author of the *Deerfoot Series* was Edward Sylvester Ellis. See *Dictionary of American Biography,* 6:102 (New York, 1931). Ed.

Chapter 8 — SPRING AT LAST! — pages 76 to 85

[1] The *Pine Knot* of July 4, 1903, reported: "Cloquet could easily be taken for a rural village or a large-sized barn yard, with cows, pigs and horses running about the street." Ed.

[2] No reports of Decoration Day ceremonies like that described by the author appear in the *Pine Knot* until 1908. In that year the paper stated on May 16 that "This is the first that Memorial Day has ever been observed here . . . and it is to be regretted that this day has been allowed to pass unnoticed heretofore." The issue of June 6, 1908, describes events as Mr. O'Meara recalls them, noting that some two thousand people were waiting at the cemetery when the parade arrived there. Ed.

[3] Bill Sarette (he was Billy Horan's uncle) operated a grocery store at Carlton Avenue and Fourth Street, although this may have been a little later than 1906.

[4] On marbles and on kites described below, see Fred Ferretti, *The Great American Marble Book* (New York, 1973); H. Waller Fowler, Jr., *Kites: A Practical Guide to Kite Making and Flying* (New York, 1953). Ed.

[5] On the Hinckley fire which killed 248 persons, see Holbrook, *Burning an Empire,* 13–30. Ed.

[6] The widely held "key log" theory described by Mr. O'Meara is disputed by William G. Rector, who dismisses it as a myth. See Rector, *Log Transportation in the Lake States Lumber Industry 1840–1918,* 256–258 (Glendale, Calif., 1953). Ed.

[7] On this ballad, see Earl C. Beck, *Lore of the Lumber Camps,* 194–197 ([Ann Arbor], 1948). Ed.

[8] The narrowest point of the St. Louis River in this area was near Thompson, at the beginning of the St. Louis dalles. A dam built there in 1907 altered the natural channel of the river. See John Birkinbine, *Report of the Water-Power of the St. Louis River,* 23–25 (Philadelphia, 1888); Minnesota Conservation Department, *The St. Louis River Watershed,* 31 (Division of Waters, *Bulletins,* no. 22 — St. Paul, 1964). Ed.

[9] Izaak Walton and Charles Cotton, *The Compleat Angler,* 40 (London, 1935). Ed.

[10] Sherman L. Coy, a 1901 Yale graduate, was in 1906 assistant manager of the Cloquet Lumber Company. During his career, he was also associated with the Northern Lumber Company. His brother, Edward H. "Ted" Coy, graduated from Yale in 1910. Rudolph M. Weyerhaeuser was an officer of the Northern Lumber Company, the Johnson-Wentworth Company, the Cloquet Lumber Company, the Northwest Paper Company, and the First National Bank of Cloquet. On the Coys, see *Alumni Directory of Yale University 1923,* 91, 138 (New Haven, 1923); Joseph A. A. Burnquist, *Minnesota and Its People,* 4:496 (Chicago, 1924). On Weyerhaeuser, see *Gazetteer, 1910–1911,* 274; *Pine Knot,* July 19, 1946. Ed.

[11] Mr. O'Meara wrote the editor that he recalls Danderine as a widely sold hair preparation whose advertisements showed twin sisters with hair that fell to their feet. According to Arthur J. Cramp, ed., *Nostrums and Quackery,* 2:73 (Chicago, 1921), it was a yellowish brown liquid with the odor of oil of bay that contained 9 per cent alcohol. Ed.

[12] The *Pine Knot* reported on October 7, 1905: "Miss Jennie Smith returned home from St. Luke's Hospital in Duluth where she has been a patient. She is much improved in health." Ed.

[13] On October 8, 1910, the *Pine Knot* reported "Miss Jennie Smith Cured" after four months of treatment in St. Paul, noting that she had "not walked without assistance for eleven years." Ed.

Chapter 9 — TO KILL A SUMMER'S DAY — pages 86 to 99

[1] For descriptions of these games, see William W. Newell, *Games and Songs of American Children,* 185, 189 (New York, 1963). Ed.

[2] These are emphatically not the true names of the gentlemen involved in this curious episode, which was, of course, a survival of the once widespread frontier custom of "posting."

[3] Joseph F. Phelion's smithy was located at the southeast corner of Vine Street and Avenue B, according to *Gazetteer, 1906–1907,* 307. Ed.

[4] On the fire and Hurtig's suicide below, see *Pine Knot,* November 23, 1907, August 7, 1909. Ed.

[5] *Pine Knot,* August 17, 1907, reported: "A great number of Cloquet people have been out during the past week picking berries. The berry crop is especially bountiful this season, blueberries being especially large and abundant. A favorite resort of the berry pickers is on the cut-over land near Pine Grove." Ed.

[6] See *World Almanac, 1907,* 286.

[7] A notice in the *Pine Knot*, June 3, 1905, reads: "A party of automobilists had one of the usual 'bubble wagon' experiences Thursday evening. They got out of town a few miles and the blame thing bucked and refused to go. Result a 'hike' in the dark and much harsh language. Can't you guess who they were?" Ed.

[8] Stokes Wilson was elected the first mayor of the city when the village of Cloquet was incorporated as a city in 1904. Before that he had been president of the village council. See *Pine Knot*, November 19, December 10, 1904. Hugo Schlenk, Sr., went to Cloquet in 1906 as office manager of the Northern Lumber Company, the first of many positions he held with the Weyerhaeuser interests there. See *Pine Knot*, July 21, 1906. Schlenk was interviewed by Helen M. White for the Forest History Foundation in 1955, and a typescript of his recollections is on file in the Minnesota Historical Society's manuscripts collection. Ed.

[9] Thomas Jefferson and John Adams both died on July 4, 1826, only eighty years before the time of which I am writing.

[10] Lengthy reports on Cloquet's Fourth of July celebrations appear each year in the *Pine Knot* for this period. Only the earlier ones from about 1903 to 1905 seem to have featured balloon ascensions. Ed.

[11] The ice cream cone is said to have been invented at the Louisiana Purchase Exposition in St. Louis in 1904. Mr. O'Meara wrote the editor in August, 1974: "I was at the Fair and remember the newly invented cones distinctly." See also Joseph N. Kane, *Famous First Facts: A Record of First Happenings, Discoveries and Inventions in the United States*, 233 (New York, 1950). Ed.

Chapter 10   — THE BIG, WIDE ROOT BEER RIVER — pages 100 to 105

[1] Near present-day Floodwood, a well-established fur trade canoe route left the St. Louis and connected with the East and West Savanna rivers by way of the grueling six-mile portage to Big Sandy Lake and the Mississippi watershed. The route is mapped and described in June D. Holmquist and Jean A. Brookins, *Minnesota's Major Historic Sites: A Guide*, 153–163 (St. Paul, 1972). Ed.

[2] The *Pine Knot* reported on July 11, 1908: "In a year or so Wm. Delyea will have no equal in the picturesque sport of 'log birling' . . . He is certainly a coming champion." Ed.

[3] Each lumber company had its distinctive log mark which was stamped with a steel hammer into each end of all sawlogs, serving precisely the same purpose as cattle brands. A few such marks used in the Cloquet area are reproduced in Mr. O'Meara's novel, *The Trees Went Forth*, 142 (New York, 1947). See also Elizabeth M. Bachmann, "Minnesota Log Marks," in *Minnesota History*, 26 : 126–137 (June, 1945). Ed.

[4] Jonas Delyea's activities occasionally made the local paper. On May 21, 1904, the *Pine Knot* reported that he "took a crew of men up the river to break a log jam." On April 27, 1907, it noted that "Jonas Delyea is the foreman of the crew that sorts the logs" at the Northern Lumber Company's upper mill. Ed.

[5] John McSweeney settled at Cloquet in 1884, according to Pelkonen, "Cloquet on Parade," 31. Ed.

Chapter 11 — SUMMER VISITORS — pages 106 to 110

[1] The *Pine Knot*, April 30, 1904, announced: "Stetson's 'Uncle Tom's Cabin' is the title of a really big company, which . . . is to appear at the Nelson opera house on Thursday, May 5th. The company comprises fifty people, including a dozen specialty artists . . . and many colored comedians, who add to the big production not a little by their spontaneous wit and clever singing and dancing. Watch for the big parade." A year earlier when the same company appeared in Cloquet, the newspaper complained on April 25, 1903: "It is to be regretted that so many of our people seem to care so little for a refined entertainment for a good local cause, but will stampede an advance sale for an Uncle Tom's cabin show." Ed.

[2] On the Walter L. Main circus, see John and Alice Durant, *Pictorial History of the American Circus*, 316 (New York, 1957). Ed.

[3] On Olaf Olson and his family, see Pelkonen, "Cloquet on Parade," 49. Ed.

Chapter 12 — THAT WAS TIMBER! — pages 111 to 113

[1] On the Idaho migrations of the early 1900s in general, see Holbrook, *Holy Old Mackinaw*, 152–160. For the Coeur d'Alene area in particular, see Ruby E. Hult, *Steamboats in the Timber*, 77–92 (Caldwell, Ida., 1952). Ed.

[2] When in 1918 a great forest fire destroyed Cloquet, the fourteen saloons on Dunlap Island as well as several mills on the mainland did not burn, including the Cloquet Lumber Company, the Johnson-Wentworth Company, and the Northwest Paper Company. Only one public building, the Garfield School, and "half a dozen houses on the south side" withstood the fire. See *Pine Knot*, October 18, 1918; Pelkonen, "Cloquet on Parade," 64. Ed.

Index

128

OTHER BOOKS BY WALTER O'MEARA

THE TREES WENT FORTH
TALES OF THE TWO BORDERS
THE GRAND PORTAGE
MINNESOTA GOTHIC
THE SPANISH BRIDE
THE SAVAGE COUNTRY
THE FIRST NORTHWEST PASSAGE
THE LAST PORTAGE
THE DEVIL'S CROSS
GUNS AT THE FORKS
JUST LOOKING
THE DUKE OF WAR
DAUGHTERS OF THE COUNTRY
THE SIOUX ARE COMING!